I0203543

Spiritual Direction
Principles and Praxis

Fr. Dominic Anaeto

En Route Books & Media, LLC
St. Louis, MO

⊕*ENROUTE*
Make the time

En Route Books and Media, LLC
5705 Rhodes Avenue
St. Louis, MO 63109

Cover credit: Sebastian Mahfood

Library of Congress Control Number:
2019944151

Copyright © 2019
Fr. Dominic Anaeto
All rights reserved.

ISBN-13: 978-1-950108-14-5
ISBN-10: 1-950108-14-7

No part of this booklet may be
reproduced, stored in a retrieval
system, or transmitted in any form, or
by any means, electronic, mechanical,
photocopying, or otherwise, without
the prior written permission of the
author.

Dedication

To Mother Abbess Patricia Alufuo, OSB

Table of Contents

Preface

When Pope Benedict XVI called for the year of faith (October 11, 2012 - November 24, 2013), he invited the people of God to seek spiritual direction, for even the most devout Catholics have questions or struggle with elements of the faith or desire more focus. Where there are those in need of spiritual direction, the Holy Spirit reaches through those able to provide it.

While we all have a secret longing, a deep yearning, for spiritual direction, the ministry of it makes even the best and most apostolic of priests, religious and lay apostles nervous. Those who are dissatisfied with spiritual direction are often so because of the kind of frustration they have experienced concerning it.

As William A. Barry and William J. Connolly point out in their book *The Practice of Spiritual*

Direction,[1] the spiritual director, who has been invited to help another Christian faithfully respond to God's Holy Will with docility and a recognition of the dynamism of the Paraclete, must have the basic qualities, which I argue are both technical and moral, to faithfully and effectively fulfill his or her role. In this book, we shall be exploring these qualities of the spiritual director.

The aim and objective of this ministry is to open our directees to the assistance of the Holy Spirit so that they may all discern how to be more fully themselves in Christ. The human director is, therefore, only the facilitator of the work of the Holy Spirit and plays a subordinate role to the Holy Spirit. Hence, the director's primary duty is to help the directee discover the Spirit of God, that is, the Holy Spirit, Who may be within him or her, hitherto unknown to the directee.

Precisely because we are created in the image and likeness of God with rational souls designed for joyful and eternal communion with our Creator, everyone has a spiritual life. Where there is spiritual life, there is opportunity to live

---

[1] William A. Barry and William J. Connolly, *The Practice of Spiritual Direction* (New York: HarperOne, 2009), 128.

it more perfectly and more fully, and that is the purpose behind spiritual direction.

As the Congregation for the Clergy explains, "In accordance with the call of Jesus ('be you perfect then as your heavenly Father is perfect' Mt 5:48), the priest invites the faithful to undertake 'the part of that fullness of life proper to the children of God' so as to arrive at 'a lived knowledge of Christ.' The demands of a Christian life (lay, religious and priestly) are incomprehensible without this 'spiritual' life or life according to the Spirit, which brings us to proclaim good news to the poor (cf. Lk 4:18)."[2]

While there are many good books available on the market that concern spiritual direction, the uniqueness of this book lies not only in the instruction it provides to the aspiring spiritual director, but also in the interaction it offers to engage in the practice of spiritual direction over the course of the reading process through role plays at the end of each chapter. By engaging in these role plays, those in preparation as spiritual directors will be more equipped in their ministry, which will help them more adequately

---

[2] Congregation for the Clergy, *The Priest, Minister of Divine Mercy: An Aid for Confessors and Spiritual Directors*, §84. Available online at http://www.clerus.org/clerus/dati/2011-05/20-13/sussidio_per_confessori_en.pdf

prepare their directees to embrace and get the best out of their time with it.

I

Definition of Spiritual Direction

Recent literature on spiritual direction reflects a fair consensus on its meaning, and a review of a couple of definitions is helpful for our study.

> Christian spiritual direction defined as help given by one Christian to another which enables that person to pay attention to God's personal communication to him or her, to respond to this personally communicating God, to grow in intimacy with this God and to live out the consequences of the relationship.

The above definition implies that one Christian (director) helps another (directee) to pay attention, to hear God's word to him or her and to recognize, to understand, what response the

Lord would require from him or her in the call the Lord is initiating. That person would then be empowered to respond generously in love because of the growing intimacy with the Lord. As a result, that person would find the capacity to live out the consequences of his or her relationship from the depth of his or her being.

It should be noted that there are three important moments of the directee's experience of this relationship, "to hear, to understand and to respond in love," during each of which the director can be of help to the directee. The experience clearly is that of the directee, not of the director, though the director's experience is also very helpful in interpreting the directee's experience. The director can help the directee to hear, recognize and understand for the purpose of responding adequately and holistically.

> Christian spiritual direction defined as an interpersonal relationship in which one person assists others to reflect on their own experience considering who they are called to become in fidelity to the Gospel.

This definition emphasizes the point that spiritual direction concerns itself not simply with the spiritual but indeed with the whole person; body, mind and spirit, and, in fact, not only with the life of prayer but also with the entire faith-life of the individual in question. In other words, the whole human being is involved: his or her every deed and attitude, thought and feeling, responsibility and relationship that uniquely constitutes him or her as a person.

It should be noted also that fidelity to the Gospel in the above definition does not primarily mean the written word but rather Him about Whom the word is written and Who is, in fact, the Word.

Christian spiritual direction is a tradition as old as the Church itself. St. Paul's first epistle to the Thessalonians might be one of the earliest foundations of this practice:

> *We ask you, brothers, to respect those who are laboring among you and who are over you in the Lord and who admonish you, and to show esteem for them with special love on account of their work. Be at peace among yourselves. We urge you, brothers, admonish the idle, cheer the fainthearted, support the weak, be patient with all. See that no one returns evil for evil; rather, always seek what is good [both] for each other and for all.* (1 Thess. 5:12-15)[3]

---

[3] Unless otherwise stated, all biblical quotations are taken from the *New American Bible, Revised*

7

As this message indicates, the practice now known as spiritual direction is a spiritual counsel given by either somebody who is "over" (in the Lord) the other members of the Church (v. 12) or by one member of the Church to another (v. 14) for the good of each other and, collectively, for the good of the whole Church (v.15).

Spiritual direction as a practice of the Church always involves a directee who is seeking truth, the Holy Spirit, Who is the primary director, and a director or a spiritual counselor through whom the Holy Spirit pleases to reveal the truth that is contained in the Treasury of the Church.[4]

As a practice of the Church, it can be said that spiritual direction is a ministry within the Church[5] that is tasked with helping the faithful to form and nourish an intimate relationship with God, such that everything they do is done

---

Edition, United States Conference of Catholic Bishop (2016).

[4] Daniel Burke and Fr. John Bartunek, *Navigating the Interior Life: Spiritual Direction and the Journey to God* (Steubenville, OH: Emmaus Road Publishing, 2012), 5.

[5] William Barry, SJ, *Spiritual Direction and the Encounter with God: A Theological Inquiry* (Mahwah, NJ: Paulist Press, 2004), 4.

in the context of that relationship, [6] in other words, with a great concern for God.

As a practice that leans on the Holy Spirit, the Sanctifier (Rm. 15:16; 2 Thess. 2:13; 1 Pt. 1:2; 1 Cor. 6:11), Spiritual Direction is intended to help members of the Church "on the journey of sanctification"[7] by means of "discernment of the Spirit."[8]

The word 'journey' implies something that is on-going. Thus, as Daniel Burke and Fr. John Bartunek posit, "Spiritual Direction is not a one-time event"[9] but an on-going communication between a director and a directee, based on trust and accountability on both sides. The director must trust the genuine intention of the directee, without which the director will be unable to focus and to respond meaningfully. On the other hand, directees who fail to trust their directors may not expect spiritual growth as they will be unable to share their experience of God, which is an important component in the practice.[10]

---

[6] Ibid., pp, 5-7.

[7] Congregation for the Clergy, *The Priest, Minister of Divine Mercy*, §66.

[8] Ibid.

[9] Burke and Bartunek, *Navigating the Interior Life*, 5.

[10] Barry, *Spiritual Direction and the Encounter with God*, 4.

Accountability[11] is required on both sides, not only because trust is built on it (one who is not accountable can never be trusted), but also because spiritual growth and spiritual "mastery" require a certain degree of discipline in spiritual practices. One who is without spiritual "mastery" cannot possibly direct another person on spiritual matters. On the other hand, a directee without accountability in practicing spiritual exercises cannot expect to grow spiritually.

Barry and Connolly's definition of Christian spiritual direction in *The Practice of Spiritual Direction* provides an adequate working definition toward a general understanding of the nature of Christian spiritual direction. In the first place, spiritual direction is necessarily a relationship between not only the director (who by the way, as the history of the Church clearly establishes, need not be a priest, but can also be

---

[11] The aspect of accountability in spiritual direction is likewise a great gift and blessing since it encourages us to not only "talk the talk," but to "walk the walk." Regular, ongoing interaction with a spiritual director ensures that we actually "practice what we preach." Not only does accountability suggest the importance of regular spiritual direction, but it also further reveals the vital importance of trust, transparency and docility between Director and Directee.

a competent and qualified religious or lay-person) and directee, but as Burke and Bartunek argue "three persons: the Holy Spirit, the director, [and] the directee."[12]

As Dubay sagely posits in *Seeking Spiritual Direction*,[13] the primary director is the Third Person of the Trinity, the Paraclete, who wills to use the human instrumentality of the secondary director to aid the directee in realizing his perfect fulfillment in the beatific vision by entering into a dynamic relationship of love with the Triune God while in this earthly life.

Accordingly, spiritual direction is necessarily focused on the directee's experience of the divine in an ongoing relationship of love with the one true God. Barry and Connolly highlight that spiritual direction, then, is not so much about understanding the relationship between the directee and God better, but "to engage in it, to enter into dialogue with God. Spiritual direction of this kind focuses on what happens when a person listens to and responds to the

---

[12] Burke and Bartunek, *Navigating the Interior Life*, 8.

[13] Thomas Dubay, *Seeking Spiritual Direction: How to Grow the Divine Life Within* (Cincinnati, OH: Servant Books, 1993).

self-communicating God." [14] Barry and Connolly's definition harmonizes with the Congregation for the Clergy's *The Priest, Minister of Divine Mercy*, which succinctly states, "Spiritual direction is not simply a doctrinal consultation. Rather it concerns our relationship and intimate configuration with Christ. This is always Trinitarian."[15]

The goal of Christian spiritual direction is not merely an attentiveness to the divine communications of light, love and grace, but a personal and integrated response that leads to intimacy with God in this life that is clearly expressed by concrete acts of virtue, especially charity, and ultimately realized in the beatific vision of heaven. Dubay summarizes that genuine Christian spiritual direction ought to "help the directee to be more and more docile to the light and promptings of the divine Sanctifier, identifying impediments to this, as well as ways to overcome them, giving instruction and encouragement in living a life of virtue, and assisting the directee to advance on the path of prayer – the road to union with God."[16]

---

[14] Barry and Connolly, *The Practice of Spiritual Direction*, 7.

[15] Congregation for the Clergy, *The Priest, Minister of Divine Mercy*, §69.

[16] Dubay, *Seeking Spiritual Direction*, 32-33.

Since the Christian life is a journey, spiritual direction ought to illumine the path and the unceasing activity of God Who is "always acting to draw us into community with the Trinity and thus with one another; this community is the Kingdom of God, and its bond is the Holy Spirit poured out into our hearts."[17] Barry herewith highlights the necessarily ecclesial dimension of Christian spiritual direction and the importance of the spiritual director firmly adhering to the one deposit of faith contained in Scripture, Tradition and the Magisterium; accordingly, just as spiritual direction is not a lecture or a homily, so, too, it is not about the director's personal opinions. Dubay pointedly stresses, "Spiritual direction can flourish only when it is solidly grounded in the ecclesial community to which that revelation [of Christ the Lord] has been committed."[18]

Spiritual direction can also be defined as a sustained attempt at leading a person to an understanding and an acceptance of self, thus helping that person strip away the barriers that impede the action of the Holy Spirit in him, that is, to a greater opening to the Holy Spirit and his movements within the person.

---

[17] Barry, *Spiritual Direction and the Encounter with God*, 5.

[18] Dubay, *Seeking Spiritual Direction*, 40.

Spiritual direction can also be defined as the help one person gives to another to enable that person to become a better version of himself or herself *in the faith*. The specific difference between the spiritual director's role and the role of a different kind of facilitator lies in these three italicized words. This is because other help studies, like therapies, can help one become a better version of himself or herself in general but not *in the faith*. In spiritual direction or through spiritual direction, one is available to the Holy Spirit in order to discern who he or she truly is *in the faith*. One cannot become himself or herself fully and perfectly except in Christ Jesus, the Son of God.

Barry and Connolly focus on spiritual direction as a process. In that sense, their definition matches well with the Congregation for the Clergy's definition as "an essential part of initial formation for the priesthood."[19]

Burke and Bartunek also emphasize that spiritual direction, as a "process," is one of developing a relationship with Christ, understanding His will in the directee's life, and determining concrete ways of living that out. Burke and Bartunek expand on Barry and Connolly's definition by stating that the person receiving

---

[19] Congregation for the Clergy, *The Priest, Minister of Divine Mercy*, §68.

spiritual direction is specifically communicating with the Third Person of the Trinity, the Holy Spirit. He states thus, "Spiritual direction is the means through which the Holy Spirit guides us and provides coaching for our souls."[20] It is ongoing spiritual (not psychological) guidance. The directee is not talking about God with a friend but is being challenged and guided by the director to grow spiritually. Burke and Bartunek's definition also includes the dimension of a three-way relationship of directee, director and Holy Spirit.

Dubay emphasizes the spiritual and relational dimensions of spiritual direction in his definition as the "guiding of a person into a life truly under the dominion of the Holy Spirit."[21] At the same time, he points out that spiritual direction should be based in the ecclesial authority of the Church and in sound interpretation of Scripture.

Barry further establishes the theological aspects of spiritual direction as an encounter with God. He notes that it "presupposes that God acts in our world in such a way that we can experience God's action." This experience is real and not purely subjective. Like the other

---

[20] Burke and Bartunek, *Navigating the Interior Life* (Kindle Locations 263-264).

[21] Dubay, *Seeking Spiritual Direction*, 32.

authors, Barry also emphasizes that spiritual direction is a relationship, not only of directee and director, but based in the Church and her broader community. Good spiritual direction needs to consider the teachings of the Church, Scriptures, Council statements and the authority of Church teaching. The relationship between directee and director will be based on these truths[22] in order to guide the directee to discern where the Holy Spirit may be speaking to him or her and operating through others. Man does not live in a vacuum. We are born into families and into society. We can encounter God through others, especially as fellow members of a Christian community. Barry states that spiritual directors help the directee "pay attention to their experience and there find that they are the object of an address, a communication by the Mystery we call God and thus called into a personal relationship with that Mystery."[23] Part of the experience is how one lives and moves and is influenced by others in the Christian community.

---

[22] Barry, *Spiritual Direction and the Encounter with God: A Theological Inquiry.* Truth enables us to abide in Christ. Subjectivism is that vacuum, which can torpedo the development of personal relationship with the mystery of God in Christ.

[23] Ibid., 2.

At the end of every chapter, a role play will be introduced. Please write down on a separate sheet of paper what you would say to your directee. Try to communicate an accurate understanding of where the directee is and where he or she wants to be. Give tentative direction as to how he or she can get there. In summary, provide both understanding and direction.

Role Play and sample of an appropriate response

A 17-year-old boy is having problems with his parents at home. He comes to your office and is extremely distressed. After about 5 minutes he states: "For goodness sake, they treat me like a child. They lay down the law: Be in by 10.30pm no later! Yes, I have a problem, but I do attempt to be responsible. It is as if they do not really trust me. They always seem to know best. At least, that is what they say. I can't wait until I am 18 to leave school. After one hour, the boy left the office to resume his school duties.

A Response: Thanks for coming to share your feelings and concerns with me. You seem to be discouraged and angry because you cannot demonstrate that you are old enough to take responsibility for yourself. It also seems that you want to prove yourself responsible enough to make your own decision. Does this seem correct? You may consider listing all the things you could do to prove responsibility and then choose one to start with that your parents could accept.

What would *you* say to your directee?

II

Difference between Spiritual Direction/ Pastoral Counseling and the Sacrament of Confession

Christian spiritual direction is regularly confused with counseling, psychotherapy and, most commonly, the sacrament of confession. In order, then, to hone our understanding of Christian spiritual direction, that we may be more effective spiritual directors by understanding our responsibilities as directors when directing and as directees when receiving direction, it is helpful to carefully distinguish between spiritual direction and these related, but distinct, disciplines.

In the first place, Christian spiritual direction is not counseling. Counseling is directly concerned with problem solving, whether it be marriage counseling which hopes to lead the spouses to mutual understanding, healing and consequently increased love, or bereavement counseling that helps in the grieving process.

While spiritual direction shares with counseling the fact that life's problems may potentially be discussed, spiritual direction seeks to aid the directee in opening him or herself to the dynamism of the Paraclete that He may transform the person in His light, love and grace. Consequently, spiritual direction is not a counseling session where the director describes five step methodologies.

Here it is helpful to recall that the primary mover is God and the purpose of spiritual direction is to respond freely and consistently to divine love. Moreover, a directee does not necessarily seek spiritual direction because he or she has a particular problem, but rather to grow in the Christian life.

No one, however, attends counseling unless he or she has some sort of issue that is being worked through. Distinguishing Christian spiritual direction from counseling highlights the reality that spiritual direction is primarily concerned with the Divine Presence, helping the directee to discern God's will in his or her life and to respond accordingly.[24]

Spiritual direction, therefore, while under the guidance of the director seeks to be docile to the Holy Ghost, must be non-judgmental and allow for spiritual growth as God wills. Unlike counseling, spiritual direction is necessarily built on the one deposit of faith wherein the theological virtues are pivotal and growth in prayer is vital. Dubay, therefore, makes the excellent remark that a spiritual director's competency necessitates that he knows when he can help, when the help needed is proper to spiritual direction and when he must give a professional referral for counseling.

Christian spiritual direction must also be distinguished from psychotherapy wherein the person's mental health is treated, and the focus

---

[24] The essence of Spiritual Direction is fostering an intimacy with God in the "heart" and mind of the Directee, so that his or her spirit does not desolate but grows and has the strength to support our mortal being, and, more importantly, that it is preserved, prepared, even beautified for our union with God. Such intimacy I think, learning from our human experience of relating with one another, requires deep love that impels us to desire closeness, sharing of experiences, and the need for giving and receiving care/attention from the one we love

is on one's mood, thoughts, and feelings in order to get in touch with one's self and function in a healthy way. Psychotherapy is a medical science and therefore its primary goal is good health.[25]

---

[25] Comparing Christian spiritual direction and pastoral counseling, Gary Moon and David Benner explain: Both deal with the person holistically. Both give attention to the interplay between the spiritual and psychological dynamics in the life of the person seeking help. Each attends to self-discovery, the physical body in relation to psychological and spiritual health, and recognizes the need to "travel the way of the unconscious in order to recover the awareness of God". Both practices give attention to a person's history. Both disciplines give special attention to personal relationships, past and present. In spiritual direction, life review is a common starting point including experiences of faith and belief, and history of religious practices. Spiritual directors teach spiritual skills and educate about resources and the use of language. Both practices work with a person's motivation. Both practices help people make decisions. Both disciplines strive to make the individual more aware of his or her unconscious self, bringing it to conscious awareness, in order to facilitate rational life choices. In spiritual direction, this is called discernment. Both practices have helping goals. Hence, both practices are centered in love for the person. "For both therapist and director, insofar as each is participating in a double process of healing

In contrast, spiritual direction seeks to aid the Christian in growing in holiness. Whereas psychotherapy is likely to prescribe medications and psychological treatments, spiritual direction will invite the directee to set aside daily time for prayer and spiritual reading while encouraging the directee's active sacramental life. Burke and Bartunek here add, "[J]ust as you would not go to a spiritual director for physical therapy, it is also unwise to attempt to deal with deep psychological issues with a spiritual director (at least with one who has not received special training in both fields). When emotional or psychological issues are serious, seek specially trained professionals for help."[26]

---

and of growth, love is the supreme requirement." (Alan Jones, 1982) Christian spiritual direction and others brings about transformation, so some benefits are derived from having both spiritual director and therapist during darker seasons in one's life for it is during such times both are very compatible even though there are some differences. And very often counseling seems to be fixing some serious problems that if left undone may lead to some emotional catastrophe. (Gary Moon and David Benner, *Spiritual Direction and the Care of Souls: A Guide to Christian Approaches and Practices* (Downers Grove, IL: InterVarsity Press, 2004).

[26] Burke and Bartunek, *Navigating the Interior Life*, 5-6.

Spiritual direction must be distinguished from the sacrament of reconciliation. Amongst the Catholic faithful, spiritual direction is most frequently confused with confession and even priests, when approached for spiritual direction, have been heard to respond, "I hear confessions from 3:30-4 on Saturday afternoons."

The Congregation for Clergy in *The Priest, Minister of Divine Mercy*, expresses the relationship between the sacrament of confession and spiritual direction writing, "The ministry of reconciliation and the service of spiritual counsel and direction are contextualized by the universal call to holiness which is the perfection of Christian life and 'the perfection of charity.'"[27] In *Navigating the Interior Life*, Burke and Bartunek expound that the cause of the confusion between spiritual direction and confession is "that there was a time when it was very[28] common for confession and spiritual direction to take place together."[29]

Spiritual direction is, however, distinct from the sacrament of reconciliation. The Lord Jesus Christ instituted the sacrament of confession for

---

[27] Congregation for the Clergy, *The Priest, Minister of Divine Mercy*, §4.

[28] Burke and Bartunek, *Navigating the Interior Life*, 5-6.

[29] Burke and Bartunek, 4.

the forgiveness of sins; accordingly, confession "on the penitent's part, consists in contrition, confession, and satisfaction and which on the priest's part, entails absolution and an invitation to greater openness to God's love."[30] The sacrament of reconciliation, therefore, focuses on how the penitent has hurt or broken one's relationship with God and neighbor.

While spiritual direction must indeed treat of sin, particularly in light of the person's eradication of vice and growth in virtue, spiritual direction's concern is broader than simply sin. Certainly, spiritual direction might reflect upon one's brokenness, but spiritual direction is ordered towards the whole person's response to the love of God, both his strengths and his weaknesses, particularly in light of the divine encounters, what we might call "moments of grace," each day. A clear manifestation of the Church's understanding of the distinction between spiritual direction and the sacrament of confession is that whereas a spiritual director [31] need not be a priest, but can be

---

[30] Congregation for the Clergy, *The Priest, Minister of Divine Mercy*, §36.

[31] The director must be particularly vigilant that he does not impose *his* or *her* spirituality on the directee, but rather that he or she helps the directee to discern how the Holy Ghost is working *in the*

deacon, religious or member of the lay faithful, the minister of confession must be a priest. In *Seeking Spiritual Direction*, Dubay makes the insightful observation that "priests who are trained to evaluate moral matters in the Sacrament of Reconciliation...[may] not understand well the higher reaches of total Gospel living, including infused contemplation and the

---

directee. When we mentor under someone, we regularly seek to make a photostatic copy of the mentor. For example, when we mentor at a new occupation, we learn the practices of that trade from another person and do as he or she did. Spiritual direction is clearly different for, as St. Therese of the Child Jesus beautifully articulated in her *Story of a Soul*, there are no two souls exactly the same and God works differently with different souls. The spiritual director, therefore, must be careful to facilitate the relationship between the directee and the Trinity without hi-jacking that relationship or forcing his ideas, preferences or spirituality on the directee, of course all the while guiding the directee according to the one deposit of faith. For example, a spiritual director would be misguided in attempting to direct a Carmelite along the path of Franciscan spirituality although a Carmelite might benefit from an experience or teaching of St. Francis that is directly applicable to the Carmelite's relationship with the Lord and Carmelite calling.

conditions requisite for growing to the summit of it."[32]

A spiritual director must have a clear grasp of the differences between spiritual direction and these other disciplines, upholding the importance and efficacy of these other enterprises that are indeed most advantageous in improving the human condition, solving problems or in the case of confession forgiving sins, but these are in point and fact distinct from Christian spiritual direction.

Meanwhile, the spiritual director must be mindful of his or her own role, as *The Priest, Minister of Divine Mercy* states to be "an instrument in God's hands, to help others discover what God desires for them in the present moment: his knowledge is not merely human knowledge." [33] Spiritual direction is undeniably distinct from the boss/employee relationship, spiritual friendship, conferences/ days of prayer, empowering workshops, self-help programs and likewise methodologies of oriental mysticism (such as those connected to Buddhism). Christian spiritual direction is distinct from all these quite simply because, as Burke and Bartunek note, "Spiritual direction is

---

[32] Dubay, *Seeking Spiritual Direction*, 43.

[33] Congregation for the Clergy, *The Priest, Minister of Divine Mercy*, §48.

about developing a love relationship with God that inevitably spills into all other areas of our lives."[34]

The purpose of spiritual direction is to learn how to heighten the awareness of God' presence and action in one's life and to make decisions based on the awareness. This is known as the discernment process. Counseling is the process, a course of action taken in form of a therapy/healing, of helping someone who wants to explore ways of coping better or overcome some issues in his or her life and surroundings.

People seek counseling for many reasons, some of the common issues addressed in counseling include coping with stress, improving mood and overcoming depression, enhancing self-esteem and managing anxiety about vocation, family etc. The aim of counseling is to enable the client to cope with personal decisions regarding his or her life, to enable the client to share his or her feelings about the issues in his life. The goal of counseling essentially may be to solve problems of life. For spiritual direction, one does not need to have a problem to embrace the ministry and the goal is not problem solving though in the course of the direction, problems may be solved.

---

[34] Ibid.

For spiritual direction to be effective, some essential points need to be kept in mind: Non-judgmental attitude from both the director and the directee, The Holy Spirit is in charge, the director should not have prior expectation of the pace of spiritual growth in each person, the direction should be asking leading questions to help the directee to clarify his spiritual experience, the director should not persuade the directee to a decision, etc.

In spiritual direction, faith in God is basic, faith development is central, deepening of prayer is important. Psychotherapy focuses more on mental and emotional dimensions (thoughts, feelings, moods and so on); spiritual direction focuses more precisely on spiritual issues such as prayer life, religious experiences and sense of relationship with God. Psychotherapy and spiritual direction may deal with the same human experiences, yet these experiences are different when seen from different perspectives. Psychotherapy sees them in the light of its aim to help a person to get in touch with himself in order to function better, to relate to others better, to form a well-integrated realistic ego. The primary aim of the therapist is health not holiness. The primary aim of spiritual direction is not health but holiness. Holiness can be infused by God even when health is absent or defective.

The sacrament of reconciliation is part of the sacramental life of the church. The focus is on sin and the ways in which relationship with God and others have been hurtful or broken whereas in spiritual direction, one has the time to look at how God has been present in the whole life, not just in the area of sin. In the sacrament, one would confess sins, but in spiritual direction, one might explore the pattern of sin and brokenness. The sacrament of reconciliation is reserved to the ordained ministers of the Catholic Church, but a qualified lay person may engage in the ministry of spiritual direction.

In both spiritual direction and the Sacraments, the priest becomes a mediator of Christ and helps to forms consciences, but a person can only receive absolution for sins through the sacrament of reconciliation. Christian spiritual direction does not bestow grace upon the recipient, but the Sacraments do. There remains a strong connection between the sacraments of Reconciliation and the Eucharist and spiritual direction, though.

Considering this, one sees how necessary it is today to form the consciences of the faithful so that they may partake worthily and fruitfully of the Eucharistic banquet and approach it in a state of grace. Confession is "an excellent opportunity" to invite people to begin spiritual direction, and it's "individual character" links the two together. Spiritual direction is one way to devote more time to forming one's conscience than is possible in confession.

While many priests provide very general spiritual direction of a sort, most often during the "counsel" portion of the Sacrament of Reconciliation, not all priests will have the gifts required to provide spiritual direction in its fullest sense. In fact, even retreat leaders or prayer group leaders are merely what Dubay calls "first cousins" of spiritual directors and may not necessarily provide spiritual direction. And while priests are the only ones who provide the Sacrament of Reconciliation, well-qualified laypeople, male or female, may provide authentic spiritual direction.

The document from the Congregation for the Clergy states that there is brief "counsel and exhortation" typically given to the penitent in confession. This is general direction in their life in the broadest sense but should not be confused with authentic spiritual direction. While all priests are called to provide information of a spiritual nature through homilies, by example, teaching, catechesis, etc., some priests are more suitably gifted than others to provide spiritual direction. These other liturgical events and spiritual aids are not to be confused with spiritual direction. So, while all priests are called to provide the Sacrament of Reconciliation, and give brief counsel during the sacrament, this is not spiritual direction.[35]

Spiritual direction involves seeking God's will through assistance which has been divinely given. Other disciplines or guidance, such as "psychological paradigms and analyses," psychological counseling or therapy, differ from spiritual direction because they are created by man.

Authentic Christian spiritual direction seeks to bring the directee into an encounter with the personal and living God dwelling within him or her, so it is not to be confused with Oriental or Eastern methodologies that bring "enlightenment" or general awareness of a vague higher power.

Recalling the general rule that authentic spiritual direction is provided by a competent, trained person whose methods are based on divinely given teachings, means or approaches, it is also not to be confused with therapy, counseling, spiritual friendships, or parenting. While spiritual direction may often touch upon emotional issues and involve a friendly

---

[35] Ibid., §41.

relationship, this is not the focus of the guidance provided by the director.

Spiritual direction is the process of accompanying people on a spiritual journey. Spiritual direction exists in a context that emphasizes growing closer to God (knowing and loving Christ).

It is a relationship between three persons, the Holy Spirit, the director, and the directed. And its focus is union with God. The main (central) aim of spiritual direction is to help guide the directed to purposefully, consistently and substantively grow in their relationship with God and neighbor.

Spiritual direction differs from pastoral counseling, mentoring and discipleship in that spiritual direction is not need-driven but focuses on the everyday experiences of the directed and the presence of God in those experiences. The agenda is revealed and guided by the Holy Spirit while the director and directed pay attention to the Spirit's leading and prompting as they talk together. The goal is for the directed to grow in experiential knowledge of God and self. The role of the director is to provide a safe, caring environment as well as to truly 'be' with and listen to the directed and to help the directed explore and sit with what God is offering. The focus of spiritual direction is not teaching or problem solving.

Spiritual direction, unlike pastoral counseling, always happens in the context of prayer and spiritual intimacy. This is where intimate engagement happens. Whereas in psychotherapy clinical distance is crucial to bring about objectivity and healing, spiritual direction discernment is based upon the intimate engagement of two people walking into the sanctuary of God that emphasizes growing closer to God (knowing and loving Christ). From this account, the general purpose of spiritual direction is identical with that of the whole economy of salvation, aiding the directed to love God with the whole heart, soul, mind and strength, and to love one's neighbor as oneself (Luke 10:27). This double love leads one to be filled with the utter fullness of Triune beauty (Eph. 3:19-20), a splendor so magnificent that the eye has not seen nothing like it, nor can we faintly imagine its grandeur (1 Cor. 2:9). Ultimately, this ushers in eternal life, the unending ecstasy of the beatific vision in the risen body. (John 6:56; 1 John 3:2)

Role Play: A twenty-one-year-old male raped his female counselor at gunpoint while engaging in her ministry of counseling. She is well known in the city and the church for her competence and has always carried herself so well.

She feared discussing this incident with anyone, but as days rolled on, she started experiencing some strange bodily reactions which sent some signals that she may have been pregnant from that brute. She quickly went to a good friend of hers who is a doctor and confirmed what she thought.

Upon the confirmation, her friend suggested abortion as the safe route. Considering all the implications of abortion and the shame of carrying a baby out of wedlock, she reluctantly agreed to the suggestion of her doctor friend.

From that moment on, everything changed: she pokes herself, hears the cries of babies all night long and is afraid of any human contact. In fact, she is almost running out of her mind.

As the male rapist could no longer stand seeing his former therapist in that messy condition and could no longer bear the trauma of his action, he decided to come to you for spiritual direction and a way forward.

What would *you* say to him as your directee?

III

Spiritual Direction and the Art of Active Listening

Active listening is giving the directee our full and undivided attention. It takes a lot of concentration and energy to fully force one's attention to the directee's verbal expression. Here, it goes beyond what is said to what is not said. Active listening prepares the director for responding empathically to his directee.

In spiritual direction, approximately 90% of the time is spent in active listening. To be effective spiritual director, one needs a thorough understanding of the dynamics of active listening. Active listening gathers all the information that can be related to the problem or goals presented by the directee. The director listens for clues to the directee's emotional and intellectual functioning. Another function that the directee listens to is the physical, that is, the energy level. The manner of feeling the story will either be flat (low energy level-depression/

excited-high energy level or boring dull tone. The tone of the directee's presentation is therefore extremely important.

The active listener listens to the themes of the directee's story. As the directee's story unfolds, recurring themes will surface. These themes may be of persecution, frustration, anger, low self-esteem or that nobody listens. The director is therefore listening with an inner ear. The director is listening not only to the words of the story, but also to recurring patterns that make up the total picture. This process takes time and the total picture will take several sessions to be fully appreciated. Active listening must initially take in the basic interrogatives: who, what, why, when, where and how.

The spiritual director must seek to cultivate the skill of active listening, which is essential to effective spiritual direction. While acknowledging the reality of the internal dialogue that is part and parcel of our nature as rational creatures, we must at the same time seek to quiet this dialogue when acting as spiritual directors in order to turn our whole and undivided, non-judgmental attention to the directee.

Since prayer teaches us to speak to our loving Lord with candor, but also and perhaps most importantly to listen to His "still, small voice" (1 Kgs 19:12 *RSV*), the spiritual director sagely prepares for spiritual direction by being him or herself a person of deep prayer. Wherefore, Fr. Dennis Billy, C.Ss.R., insightfully remarks in "Spiritual Direction and the Art of Active Listening," "[T]he contemplative dimension of our lives [should] be the primary point of encounter between us spiritual directors and those seeking guidance."[36]

There are seven essential aspects of active listening, which Billy identifies as inner awareness, emptying of self, disciplined attention, passive reception, simple understanding, open acknowledgment and humble recognition. In the first place, the directee deserves our attention and focus, so we must have genuine self-knowledge that permits us to keep our passions rightly ordered and our ears, mind and heart open to not only what the directee is saying, but what he or she is not saying, as well as how the Holy Ghost desires to use us.

Kenosis, or self-emptying, therefore, necessarily follows by which we identify what aspects of our internal dialogue are self-centered, detach ourselves from all such egotism and judgment, and redirect our attention to the

---

[36] Dennis J. Billy, C.Ss.R., "Spiritual Direction and the Art of Active Listening," *Seminary Journal* 19, no. 1 (2013), 22.

directee; self-emptying is so vital to the success of direction that the director does well to frequently return to this process throughout a given period of direction.

The director's attention, then, can be fully given to entering into the entirety of the experiences of the directee as a person, seeing the whole of the person and then bringing to bear the one deposit of faith to invite the directee into ever greater divine intimacy. At the core of listening, however, is a passive reception that attentively hears and pays heed to all that the directee shares. As Billy remarks, "Passive reception is an ascetical practice that requires openness to others and a willingness to simply be in another's presence. It requires patience and longsuffering, the kind that is willing to suffer the tediousness of the present moment for the sake of a higher good."[37]

What is shared in spiritual direction by the directee must be deeply received by the director, although externally the director appears to simply be silent and focused on the words of the directee. Active listening continues by the director's collecting what has been shared from the heart and experience of the directee into a unified whole. Simple understanding, then, is remarkably simple as it is primarily intuitive

---

[37] Ibid., 24.

and born from simply hearing the directee who has made a gift of him/herself in the process of sharing his or her prayer and experiences of the divine; accordingly, simple understanding is born from the reception of this gift of self from the directee.

The directee's self-gift is cherished in the heart of the director and then openly articulated to the directee, moving from the general to the particular, void of characterizations or swift leaps, but rather gently acknowledging the directee's circumstantial experiences and seeking additional feedback and guidance from the directee. In this way, the directee is empowered and a mutual understanding is arrived at, but this necessitates humility on the part of the director.

As Billy notes with great wisdom, "Only when what we have expressed has been received—and accepted—by those seeking guidance can we be confident we have under-stood them [the directee] correctly."[38] Although the director's acknowledgment may at first be difficult for the directee to receive, the directee will come to see the truth of the director's understanding of the experience and accordingly. Now the directee must acknowledge the fruit of direction and accept

---

[38] Ibid., 25.

the truth that has been brought to the experience, moving them to act or renewed reflection. Billy thoughtfully adds that by being listened to, the directee is learning in turn how to listen, whether to God or to neighbor, in the future.

Undeniably, listening is a skill that must be acquired through practice. Through repeated efforts at active listening, the director becomes a better listener and thereby a more effective spiritual director. Peer groups can aid the director in acquiring and growing in the skills of active listening, particularly through critiqued training sessions of spiritual direction. Again, the director becomes a better listener by seeking to grow in the spiritual life himself, particularly contemplative prayer by which he learns to listen to the Lord. Accordingly, active listening, born from our lives of prayer and returned as a gift to the directee who has given us a gift in his shared experiences, enriches the whole of the Christian life.

Active listening [39] may seem to be an insurmountable task, but it can be accom-

---

[39] The key to active listening is learning to sort out what thoughts belong to the direction session and which ones do not. This is part of the self-emptying.

plished with years of disciplined practice. One will never listen perfectly, but the effort will help to build up a relationship between spiritual director and directee that will achieve the greater good of both involved and ultimately become an essential building block of authentic spiritual direction. Billy notes that those seeking guidance "may not like what is reflected back to them," or that they might "react against it."[40] This speaks of the intriguing role of listening in spiritual direction, and that through speaking, one can truly reach deeper insights about one's relationship with God.

When a listener is truly discerning, he or she might "read between the lines" and hear more than what is just being "said" by the directee. In this case, the director can repeat back more than what was said. When the director summarizes

---

However, spiritual direction might best take place in a private atmosphere. One might be distracted by an uncomfortable feeling that someone could walk into the sanctuary at any time. Hence, part of the preparation for good active listening would be to find a quiet, private location. For priests providing direction to a woman, this might also entail a closed glass door, or semi-private place for the sake of avoiding scandal or temptation.

[40] Billy, "Spiritual Direction and the Art of Active Listening," 25.

or paraphrases what's been said, the directee will hear it said a different way and perhaps see things from a different perspective. Hence, summary and paraphrasing in spiritual direction is for clarity in the mind of the directee.

Role Play:

A divorced man is estranged from his adult children and is stuck at home when a bad car accident leaves him unable to walk. The insurance and disability payments cover his financial needs, but he is so terribly lonely. He signed up for meals-on-wheels, but the person delivering gets impatient because the man takes so long to get to the door. He won't stay to visit for even five minutes and just drops off the food and leaves. After a few weeks, the divorced man has convinced himself that no one cares about him and it would be better for everyone if he committed suicide. Still thinking about all these, he comes to you for direction.

What would *you* say to your directee?

IV

The Objective of Spiritual Direction

Spiritual direction is orientated toward holiness since God calls each man and woman to holiness by entering a relationship with the Blessed Trinity in this life for the purpose of receiving the beatific vision in the next. Without due regard for holiness, spiritual direction becomes meaningless.

Consequentially, spiritual direction is ordered toward aiding the directee to know, and more importantly, respond to the dynamism of the Paraclete in the directee's life. We might say that spiritual direction's sole purpose is to help the directee grow in docility to the activity of God and to the graces He seeks to bestow on the directee.

Such docility, of course, is the fruit of a mindfulness of the unfailing Divine Presence; therefore, attention to the Presence of God must necessarily be a primary area of attention in

Christian spiritual direction. When we are attentive to the activity of God in our lives, we seek to know and to do His perfect will, which is nothing less than discernment.

A word on discernment is helpful since there can be a false understanding of discernment. We do not simply need to discern our personal vocations, as critical as this type of discernment and spiritual direction is, but we need to be constantly seeking to discern God's will throughout the whole of our lives so that our wills might be wholly conformed to the Divine Will.

Quite simply, discernment does not end when we are ordained, profess perpetual vows, or are married, but it is rather the work of a lifetime with which spiritual direction is primarily concerned. A secondary, important note on discernment is that the director ought to strive to respect the legitimate charisms and gifts that have been bestowed by God on the directee, never imposing the director's will, spirituality or ideas on the directee.

Spiritual direction is robbed of its meaning, moreover, if it does not respect the dignity of man as a free creature. Therefore, as *The Priest, Minister of Divine Mercy* acutely observes, the directee must take responsibility for his actions. The director cannot and must not force the directee, but rather encourage the directee to freely and generously correspond to the promptings of the Holy Ghost in the directee's life, seeking an ever richer, more dynamic and intimate relationship with the three Persons of the one true God.

To accomplish the main objective of spiritual direction, "to discern the signs of God's will,"[41] the spiritual director must help the directee remain open and docile to the Holy Spirit. The directee should be seeking holiness. It seems best that the spiritual director should first ensure that the directee is motivated by this goal before spiritual direction begins. Remaining compliant and submissive to the Holy Spirit involves a certain level of practice of the virtue of humility.

Not only must the spiritual director engage in active listening, but the directee should also open up to and become aware of the Holy Spirit's direction and communication. This process is called discernment. The more one prays and progresses in the spiritual life, the clearer this process may become. Dubay asserts that one's faithfulness and charitable works will increase the activity of the Holy Spirit in one's life. "What careful investigation discloses is

---

[41] Congregation for the Clergy, *The Priest, Minister of Divine Mercy*, §78.

that, while the Spirit does enlighten the disciples, his wisdom is given to the extent of their fidelity to the Church's teaching and their generosity in living the Gospel message. Saints abound in divine light; sinners do not."[42]

St. Joseph comes to mind as a holy man who was clearly docile to the Holy Spirit. Scripture says very little about him, and we never hear him speak. This implies he was a man who listened to God more than he petitioned God. St. Joseph is described as "just" and is obedient to the commands of the angel who appears to him several times. Scripture reveals that St. Joseph and Mary discerned in their role as parents to Jesus, as they wondered "over all that was said of him." (Luke 2:33).

The *principal* objective of spiritual direction, or the one goal that must be achieved with or without additional intention, is the discernment of the will of God *for* our journey of vocation, prayer, perfection, for our daily life and for our fraternal mission.[43] We can also say that the principal objective of spiritual direction is discernment of the will of God *through* our journey of vocation; **that is, *through* our living the life that God is calling us to live, *through* our**

[42] Dubay, *Seeking Spiritual Direction*, 268.

[43] Congregation for the Clergy, *The Priest, Minister of Divine Mercy*, §78-80.

proactively engaging our prayer lives and *through* our intentionally pursuing our journey to perfection by keeping an unceasing desire for holiness and submitting to the concrete action toward it, *through* our maintaining awareness of every event that makes up the day, *through our* being fully present in body, mind, and spirit throughout our experiences of each day, and *through* our cultivating and nurturing our relationship with other people as Christ bearer to one another. All these are manifestations of a Christian life with sensitivity to the Holy Spirit, Who is the primary Director in every spiritual direction.

In its literal sense spiritual direction is a movement toward God, our Heavenly Father, and the Gospel tells us that such movement can only be accomplished by abiding in Christ through docility to the guidance of the Holy Spirit. In the Gospel of John, after telling us not to be troubled and assuring us that He will come back again and "take [us] to myself, so that where I am you also may be" (Jn. 14:3),[44] our Lord tells us about the way to the Father, saying: "I am the way and the truth and the life. No one comes through the Father except through me." (Jn. 14:6) He then continues and says: "I will

[44] Burke and Bartunek, *Navigating the Interior Life*, 5.

send (the Advocate) to you... when He comes, the Spirit of Truth, He will guide you to all truth." (Jn. 16:7, 13).

The practice of spiritual direction is the norm of the Church for training its members to attain sensitivity to The Advocate. This training is offered and delivered by those who have previously been trained and have been practicing the way of the truth more aptly and diligently to those who, by the Holy Spirit, are led to them as a tradition that maintains holiness among the members of the Mystical Body of Christ.

The whole goal, objective, aim and purpose of spiritual direction is docility to the Holy Spirit. Hence, the whole meaning of spiritual direction is geared toward a greater openness, docility and availability to the Holy Spirit. Docility to the Holy Spirit in other words means awareness of the presence and action of the Holy Spirit within an individual so that he can support the movement and direction of the Holy Spirit in him. The awareness of the presence and action of the Spirit put in another word is discernment. Therefore, if the goal of spiritual direction is docility, the heart of spiritual direction is discernment.

It is releasing the spiritual dynamism of the person directed for maximum growth as a person and as a Christian. The immediate consequence is that there can be no true spiritual direction except with a person who has attained already some degree of inner freedom. One cannot begin spiritual direction strictly called without that inner freedom from the directee. Having established this inner freedom, then the spiritual director will confront his directee with the degree of freedom he has to help him grow in that freedom towards God, in the availability to God.

It's almost as if the spiritual director is really being Christ to the directee. Jesus sometimes exemplified the ultimate spiritual director. He really observed the actions of others, meeting them where they were. Consider the woman at the well. He of course knew her heart, knew her sin, knew her soul and everything about her, but he recognized the importance of listening to her, of dialoguing with her. Letting her tell her story, he enabled her to get in touch with what the Holy Spirit was whispering to her.

There are three stages involved in any authentic spiritual direction if the director will confront the directee with the degree of freedom that he has. He must make sure that the directee understands and accepts the amount of freedom he has. This understanding and acceptance will help him open up to a greater degree of freedom.

So, the three stages are as follows: 1) self-understanding, 2) self-acceptance, and 3) self-opening to the Spirit.

Christian freedom can be captured from two dimensions: The growing freedom **from** in other to be free **for** God. It is freedom from all the blocks and obstacles increasingly under the action of the ever-coming God to become more and more free for God or more docile for God. The Blessed Virgin Mary is the real type and figure of the Church from these two dimensions of freedom (LG chapter 8).

Lumen Gentium summed it up in the mystery of Annunciation when Mary with all the power and energy of her liberty and freedom places herself totally at the disposal of God. This is also called Active Receptivity, when Mary is free for God.

Spiritual direction for one who has yet to hear God's call and has yet to choose a vocation will be different from one who has already done so. A pastor may be in need of guidance with decisions about his parish, but a single woman in her 20s may need assistance with discerning God's call to become a religious sister or not.

Everyone is called to a life of prayer. Certainly, one could say that God is always calling people to a more active prayer life. Discernment might be necessary to determine the way in which one might pray, or for what petition or concern on which one might need to particularly focus. The prayer one does outside spiritual direction may be enriched or made more effective by revelations received during the sessions.

Therefore, spiritual direction reshapes and re-energizes one's maturation to the economy of the Spirit, conforming in obedience to the fullness of life, embodied in the triune relationship shared by the Father and the Son with the Church.

Role Play:

A woman in her early forties is experiencing a breakup in her marriage. She has searched different parishes for the right priest to hear her story. She is not looking for direction or even ways of repairing the marriage but instead has it in her mind that good men can only be found in the priesthood.

The woman, seeking comfort from a gentle male figure wants to be accepted by a certain priest and is eager to please him by bringing baked goods with personal notes of support for his work in priestly ministry to the rectory after normal working hours.

The priest is becoming concerned about these gifts and comes to you as a good friend and mentor for direction.

What would *you* say to your directee?

V

The Technical and Moral Qualities of a Spiritual Director and Directee

"God is love" (Jn 4:8). As God is in his being, so he is in his operations. The starting point and centre-piece of any understanding of the redemption won for us by Jesus is found in the heart of Jesus, opened for us on the Cross. The qualities expected by a good spiritual director are based on Christological principles. First, the spiritual director will endeavor to acquire the merciful heart of Jesus so that he or she truly becomes another Christ who is merciful and compassionate. Of course, we don't want to neglect the fact that certain human qualities that are necessary for this type of ministry are also very important for the spiritual director. Let us reflect on the human qualities of a good spiritual director.

The Priest, Minister of Divine Mercy teaches that the spiritual director should have a great welcoming disposition. He should be able to listen both patiently and responsibly. He should have a fatherly and friendly approach. He should be humble since this is a characteristic of all who offer the service of spiritual direction. He should avoid giving any impression of authoritarianism, personalism, paternalism which induces affective dependence, haste or wasting time pursuing secondary questions.[45]

These are some of the good qualities that a spiritual director can imbibe. A spiritual director should be humble enough to ask for more information and to help the directee understand the causes of his or her worries or confusions. The spiritual director can merely listen empathetically and offer some encouragement to the directee, but sometimes he might need to show empathy to better appreciate the state of the directee. The spiritual director should also develop the skills of helping people see the consequences of their state in life, whether spiritual or social and to help them realize that God is not harsh, but merciful.

---

[45] Congregation for the Clergy, *The Priest, Minister of Divine Mercy*, §101.

Secondly, the spiritual director needs to pass through "Psycho-spiritual" formation, which means that he or she needs to be psychologically and spiritually balanced since some encounters will be complicated for him or her to handle. For example, the theological doctrine concerning Christian perfection, especially regarding such questions as the essence of perfection, the obligation to strive for perfection, the obstacles to perfection, the types of purgation, and the means of positive growth in virtue.

He or she should have a detailed knowledge of the grades of prayer, the trials God usually sends to souls as they advance from the lower to the higher degrees of prayer, and the illusions and assaults of the devil that souls may encounter, like the "Dark Night of the Soul" by St. John of the Cross.

He or she needs to be well versed in psychology so that he will have an understanding of various temperaments and characters, the influences to which the human personality is subjected and the function of the emotions in the life of the individual. He or she should also know at least the basic principles of abnormal psychology and psychiatry to be able to recognize mental imbalance and nervous or emotional disorders and to be culturally sensitive.

If the human qualities are right, then the spiritual director now needs to unite those knowledge or skills in conviviality with the Trinity. These human qualities are to be model on the Trinitarian love operation. It is a love relationship; therefore, in spiritual direction there should be no room for "throw-away" culture. God the Father never "throws-away" his children; rather, he embraces them just like the story of the prodigal son. As the Psalmist says, "If you O Lord should mark our guilt who will survive. But with you is found forgiveness, for this we revere you" (Ps 130:3-4). It is the blood of Jesus, which makes us one and brings us peace (Col 1:20). Through the imitation of Christ, the spiritual director may grow in faith, hope and charity. The reality of the knowledge of God and the nothingness of man is fundamental for the spiritual life, and "it creates in the soul a profound humility that nothing can disturb; it places the soul in an attitude of truth which attracts all the gifts of God." (St Angela of Foligno).

When the Holy Spirit becomes active in our lives, He makes us more aware of our vocation. John Henry Newman expressed it this way: "I am created to do something or to be something for which no one else is created; I have a place in God's counsels, in God's world, which no one else has; whether I be rich or poor, despised or esteemed by others. God knows me and calls me by name. God has created me to do him some definite service. He has committed some work to me which he has not committed to another." This is what spiritual direction seeks to achieve as the directee strives toward the life of holiness and the Holy Spirit is constantly at work within us. The more we obey the promptings of the Spirit, the more teachable we become and the more richly the Holy Spirit dwells within us.

Since the spiritual director has been invited to help another Christian faithfully correspond to God's Holy Will with docility and to recognize the dynamism of the Paraclete, it is, therefore, necessary that the spiritual director have basic qualities to faithfully and effectively fulfill his or her role. *The Priest, Minister of Divine Mercy* identifies the profile of a spiritual director to contain the following: general personality traits of the director, practical and theoretical knowledge he or she ought to possess and the relationship between him or her and the directee.

The director must be of affable character, making the directee feel welcome and encouraging the directee to speak candidly with him. As we discussed in earlier weeks, the spiritual director must be always seeking to grow in the skill of active listening. Moreover, the spiritual director should seek to foster a healthy humor that can see God's goodness and love in even the most difficult of situations. Perhaps most importantly, however, the spiritual director should be noted for his or her humility, being discreet and attentive to the directee after first learning how to be a good father/mother from being a good son/daughter to the Church and to his or her own director.

As Barry and Connolly sagely note in *The Practice of Spiritual Direction,* "In the Christian tradition what directors most basically bring to the relationship with directees is their membership in the Christian community and their sharing in the faith of that community."[46] Humility also recognizes when the directee will benefit from professional mental health services or other services outside of spiritual direction and is not afraid to make those referrals. The director should be striving for personal holiness and be intimately familiar with the practice of spiritual direction from having first received direction him- or herself.

In order to aid the directee in the pursuit of holiness, the spiritual director must necessarily have acquired the practical and theoretical

---

[46] Barry and Connolly, *The Practice of Spiritual Direction,* 128.

knowledge to know the doctrinal truths of our faith, particularly concerning the soul's progression in prayer. Ss. Teresa of Jesus and John of the Cross repeatedly expound upon the great harm that is done to souls by spiritual directors who are ignorant of spiritual theology for want of learning. This does not, of course, mean that the spiritual director must be a world-renowned intellect, or that he or she is some sort of guru, but rather quite simply that he or she possesses sufficient knowledge to guide the directee along the paths of prayer.

Since spiritual direction is more efficacious when it is consistently undertaken over time and with one director, if possible, the relationship between the director and directee is vital to the success of spiritual direction. Over a long time, the director is able to come to know the directee very well and therewith to be able to more advantageously help the directee to grow in authentic holiness and overcome vice. Necessarily, the fostering of such a relationship of openness, trust and mutual respect takes time and requires humble docility and prudence on the part of not only the directee, but also the spiritual director.[47]

---

[47] The relationship between the spiritual director and directee, grounded in our holy Catholic Faith and necessarily built upon mutual trust and respect,

In *The Practice of Spiritual Direction*, Barry and Connolly make a final practical suggestion that seems obvious but is of the greatest importance: spiritual directors need friends who are not their directees. Why? The spiritual director, in order to effectively listen to and aid in the process of Christian discernment must possess unselfish love; he cannot be seeking his own self-affirmation through the process; rather, he must make a generous gift of himself with confidence that the Holy Ghost is at work in spiritual direction. If this bridge is crossed, the spiritual director finds himself unable to make the sometimes unpleasant, yet necessary charitable and fraternal, corrections to urge the directee on to greater heights of holiness.

---

would become unhealthy if it became physically, sexually or emotionally dependent. If the relationship were to go in this direction, "the relationship should be terminated immediately." (Burke and Bartunek, *Navigating the Interior Life*, 44). If you found yourself getting emotionally attracted to the directee, humility suggests that you would need to end the relationship since at that point not only would you be putting yourself and your vocation in a potentially dangerous situation, but just as important, your ability to help the directee to discern God's Will and to enter into an ever richer relationship with the Triune God, would no longer be able to be objective and disinterested.

Considering the qualities of a spiritual director, one can be tempted to think, "Who is truly capable? Is this beyond my capacity? I am not yet a saint, but this sounds a lot like a canonization checklist..." Here, it is helpful to recall Burke and Bartunek's solid wisdom in *Navigating the Interior Life*, "Spiritual directors are human and imperfect, and a directee might find that a director has strengths and weaknesses in these areas of responsibility. The good news is that if we understand how spiritual direction can and should work, we can help ensure that the process is as fruitful as is possible even with the normal weaknesses that crop up on both sides of the relationship."[48]

Spiritual Directors are to guide their directees to reach union with God by loving Him with all their heart, soul, and mind (Mt. 22:37); that is, through living in accord with the words of God (Jn. 14:23-24). A good guide is one who himself has reached a destination and dwelled long in it, is very familiar and feels at home in the destined place, knows how to get there from different direction and has learned from his or her own experiences the advantages and the difficulties that may be expected from taking one path or another. Similarly, Spiritual

---

[48] Burke and Bartunek, *Navigating the Interior Life*, 43.

Directors must have great love for God and the Scriptures. These two are the foundation on which certain characters naturally develop, which are suitable for screening and mentoring spiritual conscience.

True love for God inspires love for others whom God loves equally. It also inspires love for His commandment. Spiritual Directors are expected to devote full attention to the person who is confiding his or her life stories to him or her and to accept him or her "as is," without analyzing and judging.[49] The Congregation for the Clergy adds that Spiritual Directors are to "have a great welcoming disposition" and be "able to listen both patiently and responsibly" and to also have a "fatherly and friendly approach." They are also to "avoid giving any impression of authoritarianism" and avoid being "haste or wasting time" in relating with their directees.[50]

All of these are expressions of *unconditional love for others.* Further on, the Congregation also lists being humble, prudent and discreet as the qualities demanded of Spiritual Directors; also to have profound respect for the conscience

---

[49] Billy, "Spiritual Direction and the Art of Active Listening," 22-26.

[50] Congregation for the Clergy, *The Priest, Minister of Divine Mercy*, §101-105.

of the faithful, and to always act with respect and delicacy (exercising confidentiality and sensitivity) while maintaining spontaneous openness and good humour, so as to encourage ease and trust and to disperse any sense of inferiority in the directee. [51] "Without spontaneity, 'commitment and effort to understand will appear cold, impersonal, and stereotyped.'"[52]

Spiritual Directors must maintain an attitude of humility and trust that leads to prayer and to the ability of not being discouraged when he or she is unable to see the fruits of his or her labors. This includes having the wisdom even to "withdraw," by admitting his or her limitations and recommending directees to seek direction from another director for their own benefit, that is, for further advancement of their spiritual growth. It should be noted, however, that in general a sustained director-directee relationship should be maintained to ensure continuity.[53]

The issue of trust also has to do with outstanding reputation of a Spiritual Director

---

[51] Ibid.

[52] Barry and Connolly, *The Practice of Spiritual Direction*, 133.

[53] Congregation for the Clergy, *The Priest, Minister of Divine Mercy*, §101-105.

among the faith community, which must be underscored. "The more conscious directors are of the life of the Christian Community and the more knowledgeable they are about the experienced relationship of that community with God and all reality, the more helpful they are likely to be to directees."[54]

Such conscience and knowledge of God's relationship with His people, which takes form in many different ways, can only be attained through strong devotion to the Word of God that is fully contained in the Scriptures and through "a deep faith in the desire and ability of God to communicate with people."[55] Such knowledge, confidence and faithfulness to the Scriptures refers to what our Lord means when He says that those who love Him keep His words quoted in the Gospel of John above.

Personal experience of God's love, mercy and power to save from every undesirable situation, be it resulting from sins, negligence, ignorance, or the work of enemies, is very important for Spiritual Directors, as such experience brings "an attitude of quiet trust that

---

[54] Barry and Connolly, *The Practice of Spiritual Direction*, 128-129.

[55] Ibid., 130.

God will do similar things for others,"[56] without which their work has no meaning.

Perhaps no writer has outlined with great clarity and precision the technical qualities of a good spiritual director as have St. Teresa of Avila and St. John of the Cross. Both state that a good spiritual director should be learned, prudent and experienced. While not primarily a physical or mechanical process, spiritual direction can still be said to involve technical (specialized professional, scholarly, vocational or scientific) skills. When seeking an understanding of the practice and skills involved with spiritual direction, it's helpful to be aware of the technical qualities that are expected of a good spiritual director.

A spiritual director should have "a sufficient knowledge (theoretical and practical) of the spiritual life as well as experience of this and a good sense of responsibility and prudence. [57] The director is following the action of the Holy Spirit so would offer careful, discreet direction.

Additionally, a good spiritual director also understands the breadth and limits of his or her power and the awesome responsibility of that power. Spiritual directors should know their directees well, ensuring more open dialogue.

---

[56] Ibid. p.131
[57] Ibid.

This will involve topics like personal sin. "The exercise of the power of jurisdiction in the Church should always respect the reserve and the silence of the spiritual director."[6] The director has authority in terms of the counsel and guidance that they provide to the directee. They should have fidelity to Catholic teachings but are not directly involved in jurisdictional decisions regarding their directee.

Dubay talks at great lengths about all the various questions that are asked during spiritual direction. While it's impossible to be prepared for all of them given the wide variety of human experience, he says that a competent spiritual director knows where to find the answers and where to look for further study. Resourcefulness is key to being a spiritual director, as are habitual study and "a continuing assimilation of information combined with experience and sound judgment in using it."

St. Teresa of Avila highly valued theological competency as an essential characteristic of spiritual directors. A good spiritual director is also academically competent with familiarity in all areas related to spiritual direction, especially: prayer (regular and contemplative), Biblical matters, interpersonal relationships, vocational issues, morality, evil and suffering, psychological wounds and spiritual reading.

Not only should a good spiritual director have knowledge of interpersonal relationships, he or she should have these personal skills themselves. Directors should be highly accomplished in listening, docile and accepting of another's experience and emotions, and highly tolerant of the expression of those emotions. They should also ideally be a member of the Christian community in which they are directing. [58]

The learning of a spiritual director should be extensive. In addition to having a profound knowledge of dogmatic theology, without which he would be exposed to error regarding matters of faith and of moral theology, the spiritual director should have a thorough knowledge of ascetical and mystical theology. He or she should know, for example, the theological doctrine concerning Christian perfection, especially regarding such questions as the essence of perfection, the obligation to strive for perfection, the obstacles to perfection, the type of purgation and the means of growth in virtue. He or she should have a detailed knowledge of the grades of prayer, the trials God usually sends to souls as they advance from the lower to the

---

[58] Barry and Connolly, *The Practice of Spiritual Direction.*

higher degrees of prayer and the illusions and assaults of the devil that souls may encounter.

The Church has always required that all those who will be taking the duty of leading people to heaven, especially in spiritual direction, should be and must be very well educated. Souls are so valuable that need all the preparation to deal with them. St John of the Cross says that this knowledge should lead to Christian perfection. Saint John Paul the Great said that if someone is asked to be a spiritual director, but he or she knows himself or herself to be bereft of the skills, he or she should be humble and send this person to another one who is better in this matter.

The spiritual director needs to be well-versed in psychology so that he or she will have an understanding of various temperaments and characters, the influence to which the human personality is subjected and the function of the emotions in the life of the individual. He or she should also know at least the basic principles of abnormal psychology and psychiatry to be able to recognize mental unbalance and nervous or emotional disorders. The spiritual director must have good knowledge of the Sacred Scriptures. To underscore that idea, it is most important for a spiritual director to have an ample study about the sacred scripture. Saint Jerome says that "ignorance of the Scripture is ignorance of Christ."

Prudence is a virtue of practical reason and is directed particularly at the proper exercise of the moral virtues. In the natural order, prudence is a virtue acquired and practiced through trial and experience. In the supernatural order, prudence is infused at baptism and exercised through sanctifying grace. This quality will help the spiritual director to act and speak at the right moment and at the right time. In any decision, it is always important to act with prudence.

In spiritual direction, prudence consists of three basic factors: prudence in judgment, clarity in counseling and firmness in exacting obedience. The director is not called upon to make decisions regarding general doctrine; most people could find such answers in any standard manual of spiritual theology. The director's role is precisely to recognize the circumstance of a given situation and to offer help at that moment. In other words, for the help to be effective, the director must have the empathy by which he is able to place himself in the given circumstances and must have the patience to listen attentively.

In the area of counseling, the spiritual director cannot be wondering on what to say. He should be clear. So that he may be clear in his direction, he must possess clarity in his mind. In speaking to the soul he is directing, he should avoid vague or indecisive language.

If a soul perceives that the director is not sure of himself, it will lose confidence in him and his direction will lose all its efficacy. Firmness implies that the director should always be sincere and frank, without any partiality or selfish motives. Having a sense of self-confidence is vital for a spiritual director for good listening. Self-control and a patient ear are essential for trust and openness to flourish thereby encouraging directees to reveal what's in their heart and on their mind. In fact, spiritual directors are more apt to identify with directees if they themselves have experienced similar tragedies or difficulties and have sought for spiritual direction themselves. Spontaneity and a sense of warmth with a sincere desire to communicate relax both parties to drop any pretense so that the root of the difficulty can be recognized and dealt with carefully.

Experience is one of the most precious qualities of a good spiritual director. St. John of the Cross says that even if the spiritual director is less perfect in knowledge and somewhat deficient in prudence, experience can make up for these deficiencies. He maintains that there are many different paths by which the Holy Spirit can lead souls to the summit of sanctity. It would be a serious mistake for a director to attempt to lead all souls along the same path and to impose on them his or her own personal experiences, however beneficial they may have been for himself.

Every spiritual director should never forget that he or she is merely an instrument in the hands of the Holy and that his or her work must be entirely subjected to the Holy Spirit. A good spiritual director ought ideally to have grown to such a degree of holiness to have had some experience with the beginnings of infused prayer. The director can then recognize this prayer in his or her directee's experience, understand the situation and guide accordingly. St. John of the Cross also stressed familiarity with infused prayer, along with sound judgment, as important personal qualities of a spiritual director.

The moral qualities indispensable for a good spiritual director are piety, zeal for the sanctification of souls, humility and disinterestedness. If the soul has an ardent desire for sanctification and strives faithfully to cooperate with all the graces God bestows, it will not fail to reach sanctity even if the spiritual director does not possess all the qualities that are necessary.

Indeed, such a soul could possibly attain perfection even without a spiritual director. It is not the director who makes saints; sanctification is essentially the work of God and the cooperation of the soul.

It is easy to understand the necessity of piety in a spiritual director, and St. John of the Cross insists upon this quality with great emphasis. The piety of the spiritual director should be permeated with the great truths of the Christian life. It should be eminently Christocentric and oriented to the glory of God. The director should likewise be animated with a profound sense of our adoptive filiations so that he can see God above all as a loving Father. He should have a most tender affection for Mary, the Mother of God and our Mother. He should practice recollection and be detached from the things of the world. A director who is animated with these sentiments will be perfectly at home in the direction of souls. He will understand their language and will be able to communicate with them. His own experimental knowledge of God and divine will give him understanding that no acquired science could ever provide. The director's ardent zeal for the sanctification of souls is a natural consequence of his personal piety.

Zeal, as St Thomas explains, is an effect of intense love. The love of God impels us to labor for the extension of his kingdom in souls, and the love of those souls enables us to forget ourselves so that we think of nothing but of sanctifying them in and for God. This is the zeal that urged St Paul to become all things for all men in other to gain all and gave him that beautiful sympathy by which his whole being was united with others in their joys and suffering (cf 1 Cor 9.22).

Lacking this ardent zeal, spiritual direction will lose its power because the director himself will have lost the stimulus for persevering in his efforts despite any difficulty and the direction will become an oppressive burden. Zeal, however, is always in danger of degenerating into a stubborn inflexibility that would be most harmful to the person who is being directed. For that reason, it must be counter balanced by a basic goodness and sweetness of character.

The spiritual director should be animated by the same sentiments that animated our Lord and savior, Jesus Christ. If the director is excessively rigorous and lacks compassion, he will discourage the soul and may even cause it to abandon the work of its sanctification. The director needs compassion, especially in dealing with souls who are strongly tempted or those who find it difficult to open up to their spiritual directors. For that reason, the goodness and kindness of the spiritual director should enable him to be truly paternal in striving to form Christ in the souls who God has entrusted to him.

The director needs a profound humility, and this is for three reasons. In the first place, God resists the proud and gives his grace to the humble. Secondly, the spiritual director needs humility so that he will distrust himself when necessary and not rush forward to solve difficulties without reflection. Humility will cause him to study and meditate and consult others more learned than himself in this way, he will avoid many of the mistakes and embarrassments that befall those who are too proud to doubt themselves.

Thirdly, humility in a director attracts souls while pride repels them. In this respect also the director should imitate Christ, who said of himself that he is meek and humble of heart and that he seeks only the glory of his Father. Humility is needed to guide others toward Gospels norms and not one's own standards. The spiritual director who knows his or her place in relation to God and to others will be more equipped to give fruitful direction. This quality also helps the director to establish boundaries and be open to times when he or she doesn't understand the problem or can't help and the directee might need outside assistance.

The good spiritual director needs patience in order to listen attentively and lovingly accompany the directee on his or her journey toward increased understanding of God's will and direction. The directee may sometimes take two steps forward and one step back. The director's patient attitude will put the directee at ease, help him or her feel accepted and communicate that there is no quick fix for a lifelong pursuit of holiness.

On the other hand, the director must not have an overabundance of patience. If a directee keeps exhibiting signs of disinterest and does not seem motivated to grow in holiness or truly seek God's will, a director should not wait around endlessly for the person to change his or her attitude or approach. However, think of a personality with a tendency to perfection. These might be the types of people that are highly educated but not always possessing the virtue of patience. So, the moral qualities must go along with the technical qualities.

By disinterestedness, we mean that a good spiritual director should not seek to guide his directees because of any self-satisfaction or consolation that he would receive but simply and solely to lead them to God. St Augustine states emphatically that those who lead the sheep of Christ as if they were their own and not Christ's show that they love themselves and not the Lord. By means of this disinterested love, the director will forestall many temptations that could arise regarding pride and sensual affections and will be able to respect the liberty of the soul he directs.

Many of God's Holy People, when they think of who seeks spiritual direction would immediately assume that the person must be a saint, someone well-advanced in prayer and virtue, perhaps experiencing extraordinary mystical phenomenon, or a priest or religious. In other words, it seems that there is much misunderstanding of *both* what spiritual direction is *and* who seeks spiritual direction. This is truly unfortunate since much is to be gained from consistent spiritual direction in the Christian life and the resulting growth in communion with the Persons of the Trinity.

In the first place, the directee should be striving to have a relationship with God in prayer, to practice charity in the ordinary and extraordinary moments of everyday life, to develop self-discipline in order to grow in virtue and eradicate vice, to acquire healthy maturity as a person that is balanced and integrated, to approach God with faith, hope, and charity, to embrace those who have a different perspective or outlook with charity, and to earnestly seek to become a saint by using man's freedom to love God and neighbor.

Obviously, the directee will not immediately have all of these qualities at the first meeting, nor even after repeated sessions, but these qualities offer benchmarks, goals if you will, by which the directee's spiritual growth can be better assessed by both director and directee to determine both what is going *well* and where God is inviting the directee to continue to *grow* in his or her relationship with God and neighbor.

In *Seeking Spiritual Direction*, Dubay adds the important point that perhaps the most essential aspect of spiritual direction is that the directee is truly, freely seeking spiritual direction. Dubay writes, "The point is the degree of receptivity or readiness. Do I want truth, all of it? Really? Do I want holiness, or will I settle for a refined mediocrity? Do I covertly have my own agenda, rather than the Lord's?"[59] In other words, the directee has to *want* to receive direction, which is born from a desire to correspond to the unceasing activity of the Paraclete in one's life; quite simply, spiritual

---

[59] Dubay, *Seeking Spiritual Direction*, 90.

direction cannot be forced or coerced in any way whatsoever for then it is not *direction* at all.

Burke and Bartunek, in their *Navigating the Interior Life*, offer a nice comprehensive list summarizing the qualities of the directee: docility born out of humility, obedience, openness, the willingness to make both remote and proximate preparation, as well as the willingness to maintain continuity over the long haul.[60] I would add to Burke and Bartunek's list, in accord with *The Priest, Minister Of Divine Mercy*, a desire for integrity and divine intimacy that is concretely realized in the "means of sanctification (liturgy, sacraments, prayer, sacrifice, and examination..."[61]

From this vantage point, it is interesting to note how these same qualities are required of the director, but simply from the different perspective of being the instrument of the Holy Ghost in affording help to the directee.

The directee also has the responsibility to be open, to be honest, and to be committed to one's own growth. Being open entails being vulnerable, talking freely without hiding vital facts and information that will aid the director in

---

[60] Burke and Bartunek, *Navigating the Interior Life*, 45-51.

[61] Congregation for the Clergy, *The Priest, Minister of Divine Mercy*, §106.

discerning more technical ways of assisting the soul, having direct eye contact, proper body language, truthfulness in conscience as the spirit moves him or her to share what goes on in the mind.

The one receiving the assistance is obliged to be honest about situations and facts, knowing how to appropriately self-disclose to one's director, to trust and obey the spirit who directs both parties.

The directee must demonstrate some obedience and loyalty to the authority and the magisterium of the Catholic faith, believing in the true teachings of mother church, keeping the Lord's commandments, the laws of the church.

He or she must be baptized and actively practicing his or her faith. Being able to show love and respect is encouraged both on the directee and to the director so that mutual care and caring for one another may be upheld.

Appropriate and timely communication is of vital importance for the directee for free flow of information, through regular meetings and regular follow-ups. He or she is seeking for clarity, by being able to collaborate with God's grace, which is the supernatural nourishment so that through in-depth faith he or she remains nourished. This is demonstrated by a spirit of prayer, a heart of love and a knowledge of

Christ. He or she follows in His footsteps in every bit of life's billows and events, is a lover of the blessed sacrament, who seeks to live and grow in holiness.

He or she must have in-depth communion and a relationship with God leading to authentic wisdom and happiness. He or she is also intent on being wise as a serpent and innocent as a dove, aware of the pitfalls, courageous, and in times of trials and difficulties never gives up.

Role Play:

Sr. Mary Dolores has been transferred to a new mission after working for twenty years in a mission she loved so much. She is terribly sad to leave because she loves her students and co-workers very much. She is so immersed in her sadness that she stops eating and begins to constantly malign her superior for making her leave. Sr. Dolores has been known for her calmness in the community, but she radically changed, becoming cranky and getting in trouble with everyone in the community. She is beginning to hate herself and so came to you her spiritual director for help.

What would *you* say to your directee?

VI

Relationship of the Spiritual Director, Directee and the Holy Spirit

The primary director in spiritual direction is the Third Person of the Trinity, the Paraclete who works through the human instrumentality of the spiritual director. For the success of spiritual direction, it is imperative that both the director and directee bear this underlying fact steadfastly in mind, trusting that God, the First Mover, is the one chiefly at work.

As Barry thoughtfully notes in *Spiritual Direction and the Encounter with God*, "Ministers, spiritual directors, and supervisors do not create the relationship with God; they help people to develop a relationship that *already exists* because God intends it."[62] Quite simply, God is the one directing and He wills to use a human director to help the directee grow in his or her relationship with the Trinity and to ultimately behold God in the unending face-to-face of heaven.

Admittedly, however, it is not always easy, either as the director or the directee, to recognize the workings of the Holy Ghost, and we can be quick to forget that God is the one Who is at work in both the soul of the directee and a given session of spiritual direction.

The fundamental reality of the Advocate as the primary director, moreover, highlights the role of the spiritual director to lead the directee to the Spirit of God, illuminating the divine action in the directee's life and relationship with God. In order to truly help the directee, the spiritual director must have a personal relationship with the one true God Who is a Trinity of Persons. Ponder, for example, the countless souls that have no idea, or quickly forget, the mysterious reality of the indwelling of the Holy Ghost by sanctifying grace.

Spiritual direction ought to shed radiant light on the Triune God's love, mercy, providence and guidance in the life of the

---

[62] Barry, *Spiritual Direction and the Encounter with God*, 100.

directee. As Fr. Dubay beautifully articulates, "The directive relationship is a fine tuning of the human harp, that the divine Spirit may play an entirely new and sublime song upon it."[63]

It is important to also point out that once the workings of the Holy Ghost have been illumined through spiritual direction, the director fades into the background with humility, if you will, so that the directee can continue and advance in this divine encounter. This does not mean that spiritual direction should be discontinued, quite the opposite, but rather is a reminder that the primary director is the Holy Spirit.

Here we again recall the importance of striving to grow in our ability of active listening in order to facilitate this divine encounter between the primary director, the Paraclete, and the directee. Spiritual direction is neither a homily nor a theology class. The example of St. John the Baptist before our Blessed Lord offers a striking witness to the humility we should seek to cultivate and to practice in each session of spiritual direction as spiritual directors, "He must increase, but I must decrease" (Jn 3:30).

The Spirit of Jesus Christ is always present in spiritual direction. It is important for the director and directee to be aware of this

---

[63] Dubay, *Seeking Spiritual Direction*, 37.

profound presence of the Holy Spirit as a principal agent in spiritual direction. St John of the Cross express it this way: "Let such guides of souls recall that the principal agent, guide and mover of souls is not the director but the Holy Spirit. They are themselves only instruments to guide the souls in the way of perfection by faith and by the law of God according to the Spirit that God is giving each one" (St John of Cross).

The reality of Spiritual direction is about sincerely committing to the presence of the Holy Spirit for inspiration, discovery and articulation of something deeper in the reality of God's grace in our lives. As the directee excels in docility to the Holy Spirit, the awareness of God's activities in the directee's experience, the challenge is to become more aware of what we already have.

St Paul said to Timothy, "I remind you to rekindle the gift of God that is within you through the laying on of my hands" (2 Tim 1:6). In spiritual direction, it is not a situation of one person telling another what to do; rather, it is a dialogue in which the directee discovers and discusses with the director the action of God's Spirit in his or her life.

Therefore, the director is only a facilitator in the process, confirming and basically validating where God is calling the directee, and they enter this mutual process through prayerful conversation in which the director and directee can be attentive to the Holy Spirit, Who is in fact, the Real Director. When we commit to spiritual direction, we dedicate and devote ourselves to an ongoing process of being attentive to the activities of the Spirit.

The Holy Spirit will move us from our familiar space to a new place where we can grow more in our relationship with God and neighbor. It is important to reflect and to ask the question, "What is God doing in my life?" The Holy Spirit continually calls us from "doing" to "being" like the story of Mary and Martha in the Gospel of (Lk 10:38-42). Mary chose listening to the instructions of Jesus over helping her sister prepare food. Jesus affirms her that she was right because only one thing is needed. The words of our Lord are life, "meaning eternal life" (Jn 6:63). Spiritual values are more important than material things. The Holy Spirit helps us through spiritual direction to discover the most important things in our life that will give glory to God. The Holy Spirit helps us to experience the unconditional love of God through the mutual yes of both the director and the directee.

It is true that most people would agree that spiritual direction means companionship (relationship) with another person or group through which the Holy One shines with wisdom, encouragement and discernment with the fellowship of the Holy Spirit. So, in Spiritual Direction we are on Holy Ground, and it is through the real and observable experiences of our lives that God reaches out and communicates to us. This happens not only through the created world and through natural and "unwilled" events, but also through the actions and love of others.

Fr. Barry explains the difference between an action and an event—an action is willed by an agent whereas an event just "happens." An agent performs an action which is typically composed of a series of events. In spiritual direction, the Holy Spirit is the principal agent of spiritual direction. It may be said that He wills to communicate to the directee and director during the session.

Reflecting on the Scripture passage above, we see that the Spirit, Love (God the source of all goodness and love), is present in a very real way through man's relationship with both God and man. Man is called to imitate God, a relation of three Persons, to create love through sacrifice and gift to others. So naturally it is through a loving relationship with/of others that a directee may experience God, the Holy Spirit, and the third person of the divine Trinity[64]. It is the spiritual director's job to help the directee discern if and when such love may be occurring in his or her life.

The spiritual director is subordinate to the Holy Spirit. It is his or her job to help expedite

---

[64] Spiritual direction is about relationships. It is about the "incarnational" divine plan. This seems to have two aspects: the Incarnation of the Son, the second person of the Holy Trinity, but also that God invites man to accept and give love both to God and to others. Man is invited to imitate Christ, perfect man. "Teacher, which commandment in the law is the greatest?" He said to him, "You shall love the Lord, your God, with all your heart, with all your soul, and with all your mind. This is the greatest and the first commandment. The second is like it: You shall love your neighbor as yourself." (Matt 22:36-39).

So, this passage from Matthew depicts this invitation from God to love both Him and others. It relates to spiritual direction because the better the relationship between director and directee and the more they have a truly loving and trusting relationship, the better they will both be able to say "yes" to the guidance of the Holy Spirit. The "governing principle" is ultimately love—and being called to that love by the Holy Spirit—to give entirely of themselves and to each other. Matthew's passage invites us to love both God and others with our entire selves.

or ease the directee into the work of the Holy Spirit in his or her life. In spiritual direction, the director's relationship with the Holy Spirit is "likened to that of John the Baptist with Jesus in the Gospel especially (Jn. 1:29-42, 3:30) and in the Old Testament, Eli and God (1Sam 3: 1-10)."[1] The director brings the directee to the Lord in a personal way, and helps the directee discover the Holy Spirit dwelling and moving within. Then the director remembers that he or she is the "friend of the bridegroom" and allows the Bridegroom's relationship with the directee to develop uninhibited.

As Thomas Green puts it, "before the Lord becomes personally real to the directee, the director's role is to bring [him or] her to the Jordan and point out to [him or] her the One who is preaching and baptizing there. After [he or] she encounters this Lord for [him- or] herself, the director must have the sensitivity to fade into the background. The director still has a role to play, but the friend of the bridegroom must have enough sense not to try to go on the honeymoon."[65]

---

[65] T. H. Green, *Spiritual Direction and the Encounter with Christ* (Notre Dame: Ave Maria Press, 2000), 48.

The relationship between the three persons (directee, director and Holy Spirit) as crucial to good spiritual direction means that it is important to start the session in prayer. This helps remind both human persons present to be receptive and open to what the Spirit may be trying to communicate.

The spiritual director helps the directee develop his or her prayer life through praying the Scriptures in order to deepen his or her relationship with the Lord. The spiritual director also helps the directee discern the movement of the Holy Spirit in his or her life. This is useful for anyone who is serious and wants to grow in his or her relationship with the Lord.

In this practice of spiritual direction, the relationship between the directee and God is primary. It is not the job of the director to reveal God's will and plans to the directee, but to help the person to interiorize and to learn experientially which voice or spirit is operating on his or her inner psychic and spiritual life. But the spiritual director must maintain his or her own prayer life while praying regularly for the directee. Listening to the Holy Spirit and to the directee is key.

Therefore, the first quality sought in a spiritual director is an overall holiness of life.

The directee needs the mediation of a holy man or woman to bring forth new life in the Holy Spirit. A spiritual director is, therefore, like a compassionate midwife, bringing forth the spiritual life and faith residing deep inside another believer.

As the director and directee individually experience this spiritual birthing procedure, they increase the joyfulness of the event as they share the encounter through communicating and relating with each other during the process. Part of the spiritual director's job is to help the directee discern what messages and thoughts are from the Holy Spirit and what are not.

Trust between director and directee is, thus, an important part of direction. The director has only the knowledge of what the directee says has been his or her experience with the Holy Spirit. So, the director really has to rely on the Spirit and His infinite wisdom in what He does or does not allow the directee to experience. We must remember they (directees) don't know that they don't know. We directors need to remember that we have received much over a long period of time but directee's may not have the "wisdom" to know that they should be seeking God as the source and summit of happiness.

So, it is important to take baby steps with individuals and not overwhelm them or scare them off. One eats an elephant one bite at a time. Slowly, through common dialogue, directors bring about introspection. It is an art and craft process.

The burning cry of the Spirit becomes a means of grace to the spiritual formation of both the directee and the director. Surrendering to God and abandoning hindrances to the working of God in one's life fosters an intimate relationship with God. Summarily, the relationships between the Holy Spirit, the director and the directee can be likened to the biblical figures as follows:

Director and Holy Spirit - Friend of the Bridegroom, John the Baptist and Christ, Eli and God.

Directee and Holy Spirit - Disciples of John the Baptist and Christ, Samuel and God.

Director and Directee - John the Baptist and his disciples, Eli and Samuel, John the Baptist before and after (the humility to accept the reality), "He must increase but I must decrease" (Jn 3:30).

Role Play: A middle-age lady comes to you with a heavy heart of guilt because of her past life of moral laxity. She is particularly depressed because she is physically no longer a virgin, but she promised God in her younger age to give herself whole and entire to Him as a loving sacrifice. She is now a good and committed Catholic who is doing everything to appease the good Lord and making up for losing her virginity.

What would *you* say to your directee?

VII

Spiritual Direction to Priests, Consecrated Religious and Laity

Spiritual Direction for priests, consecrated religious and laity is distinctive from one another in some aspects. In giving direction to a priest, we must remember his specific call and consecration to represent the Lord in his life and ministry. This inevitably involves living a life that Christ led as the Son whose "food" is to do the will of the Father, a preacher and a teacher who shares a lived knowledge of God with all and shows them the Way to the Father, a spiritual leader who does not condemn but encourages conversion by loving the sinner and witnessing piety with his own life, a healer who is compassionate to the sick and their afflicted families, a just man who is unafraid of voicing and doing what is right even if that means going against his own cultural traditions and a brother who willingly gives up his life so that his sisters and brothers may live. Such unity of life between a priest and Christ is only possible when the priest lives no longer his life but the life of Christ.

It is necessary to inquire after the priest's commitment to his ministry and what he does routinely to nurture his spiritual life so it can supply the will and the strength to persevere in his vocation. Regular gatherings with other priests are recommended on top of spiritual practices such as daily celebration of the Eucharist, daily recitation of the Divine Office, a Marian prayer and meditation on the Word of God or other spiritual reading. Gathering with other priests is important for fellowship so as to be of mutual help to one another. It is also important to inquire after the priest's relationship with his Bishop and the implementation of the Bishop's recommendation for his life plans, ongoing formation, pastoral work, etc. Such inquiries are not meant to investigate, but rather to learn of the spiritual life of the priest, by the same token also of religious man and woman, as well as the lay people, so as to "customize" a spiritual plan that is proper for their spiritual growth.

Spiritual direction for religious men and woman is similar to what is done for ordained ministers (i.e. priests and permanent deacons) but with a primary focus on the general evangelical counsels of chastity, poverty and obedience. These professed evangelical counsels are intended to make them the living image of Christ in our time through their consecration from and for the world. In addition to fidelity to these counsels, questions related to the specific charism (foundational charism) of their order/congregation and that related to their special consecration should be asked.

Lay Christians have a special place in the community where they are placed by God as the "yeast that raises the whole dough." Spiritual direction for lay people must lead to their sanctification through a deeply loving relationship with God, such that everything that they do, from thought to action performed in every situation, for the self as well as for others, is done for love for God. "Christians should be taught that they live not only for themselves, but, according to the demands of the new law of charity; as every man has received grace, he must administer the same to others."

As The Lord did while doing His ministry in the world, it is important to always remind each one of us to take the time to withdraw from our busy life to pray, to be able to communicate with Him, whose apostolate we now carry out. This opens us to being with the Father Who loves us and with the Holy Spirit, Who is our primary guide, the Advocate and Source of our strength. In fulfilling our duty with a constant awareness to please God so that His name may be glorified through our deeds, we are fulfilling our Christian apostolate while responding to the universal call to holiness: "Love one another...be perfect as your heavenly Father is perfect." (Mt 5:44,48).

Regardless of the specific call as a priest, a consecrated man or woman or a lay person, spiritual direction should be geared toward improving one's fidelity to his or her vocation and improving his or her relationship with God through spiritual practices, through personal holiness and perfection that inspire the same in others, through fellowship with other Christians and through one's readiness for carrying out the Christian apostolate. Any program/plan for one's spiritual life must be guided by a specific project aimed at a specific goal (purification, illumination, union) according to the maturity of the person counseled.

Spiritual direction is not something only for priests or religious, but for all of God's holy people. Here it is imperative to recall Christ's command, "You, therefore, must be perfect, as your heavenly Father is perfect." (Mt 5:48) How are we to be perfect, to be transformed in God and to enter more deeply into a divine life of charity? Since we are fallen and weak, prone to sin and quick to turn back, we, regardless of our distinct vocations in the Mystical Body, need the help of other Christians. As the old saying goes, "No man is an island." Spiritual direction affords Christians the help of another Christian to invite and encourage the directee to actively, joyfully and spontaneously correspond with God's grace throughout the whole of this life to arrive at the beatific vision of heaven.

The holiness to which we have been called by baptism is one since it has its source in our God Who is one. That being said, the spiritual direction given to a priest is necessarily distinct from that offered to a consecrated religious or a member of the lay faithful. This is logical enough since the challenges faced by a priest in his parish life are necessarily distinct from the crosses born by a cloistered religious or a wife with a hectic family life.

Each individual in this list is seeking to be transformed in God and to enter ever more fully into the divine life by grace, but each has a distinct vocation with different crosses. There will be much in common for sure, but there are differences, too. *The Priest: Minister of Divine Mercy* nuances this distinction very beautifully teaching, "Theological experts describe the spiritual director as one who guides in making concrete applications, inspires generosity in self-giving and proposes means of sanctification adapted to particular persons and circumstances, bearing in mind their specific vocations. Difficulties are confronted within the matrix of a serious attempt in the authentic following of Jesus."[66] At the heart of the distinct aspects of the spiritual direction of priests, religious and laity, then, is the concrete, individualized, personal application of the Gospel.

By means of the Christian help that is at the core of spiritual direction, facilitating the divine encounter in the directee, the spiritual director "contributes to personal formation in order to build the communion of the Church."[67] In a very concrete way, we see this fruit of spiritual direction manifested in the spiritual direction of those trying to discern their vocations. Spiritual direction, however, must not cease once we have discerned our vocations, but rather must continue throughout our lives: nurturing our faith, renewing our hope, and enkindling our charity.

---

[66] Congregation for the Clergy, *The Priest, Minister of Divine Mercy*, §85.

[67] Ibid., §134.

All those living out the varied Christian vocations are called to seek the guidance of the Holy Spirit in order to make God's will for their lives clear and intelligible. Yet there are distinctive aspects of spiritual direction for priests, consecrated religious and the laity that are important to consider and incorporate into its practice. Good spiritual direction will consider one's state in life and vocation and the specific mission God calls them to achieve in order to unite themselves to Him and His holy will.

The priesthood is a specific vocation to holiness as a state in life in which a man is conformed to Christ as head and shepherd of the Church by the sacrament of Holy Orders. As living instruments of Christ, the eternal priest, the priest is given special powers to offer the Sacrifice of the Mass and to absolve sins, as well as given the duty to shepherd the people of God under his care and to form them in the Word of God, all in a spirit of service. In this manner, the priest is called to realize the general call to holiness in his priesthood through pastoral charity, which is the total gift of self to the Church that follows Christ's total gift of self to the Church of laying down His life down for his flock.

Thus, in addition to realizing the general call to holiness in virtue of his baptism, the priest has a special obligation to holiness based on the sacrament of Holy Orders as one who acts in the person of Christ, the head of His Church for the spiritual edification of those whom he serves in his priestly ministry. "When a priest seeks spiritual direction, it is always necessary to bear in mind the fact that his charism and his particular spirituality has as its fulcrum "unity of life" in the exercise of the sacred ministry."[68]

Priests are the manifestation of Christ who is the bread of life for all people. Priests, by their vow and virtue, undertake the image of the incarnational nature as a humble servant. Besides celebrating daily mass and distributing the sacraments, priests also lead in adoration, direct religious formation programs, lead the parish community in praying the rosary and provide outreach counseling to the general community, to name just a few. Priests get their authenticity as spiritual directors for the consecrated religious and laity by way of liturgical tradition and the apostolic laying on of hands.

For priests, "Ministerial action is closely linked to spiritual direction."[69] As he lives out his priestly duties every day, he witnesses to

---

[68] Ibid., §110.
[69] Ibid., §101.

what the Second Vatican Council called "unity of life." Through spiritual direction, a priest is better able to follow a pastoral plan for his life and thus guide others towards God's will. As he grows in holiness, he becomes a better witness to his flock. As the priest makes real in his own life the will of God, he is at the same time fulfilling his vocation more closely united to Christ.

Guiding the faithful is a pastoral priority, especially as it concerns cultivating vocations to the priesthood and guiding and forming those preparing to become priests. Young men who grow closer to the Holy Spirit through spiritual direction will be better equipped to hear the promptings calling them to a vocation to the priesthood.

The Congregation for Clergy calls spiritual direction a "decisive aid in this constant process of openness and fidelity to all the Church and, especially, of the ministerial priesthood's actualization of the activity of the Holy Spirit."[70] It is through the priesthood that grace is imparted and enables the faithful to be strengthened for their specific calling from God.

The consecrated life is a specific vocation concerning those who observe the evangelical

---

[70] Ibid., §140.

counsels in a stable manner and by a vow or some other sacred bond give up real or potential goods for the sake of fulfilling the general call to holiness more surely and easily. They give up the good of marriage and the normal circumstance of family and social life for the greater good of loving God and the church with undivided hearts in observing evangelical chastity in a permanent manner. Moreover, they give up the good of personal ownership for the spiritual riches of the kingdom of heaven in the effective observance of the counsel of poverty. And they give up the good of the autonomy of one's will for the greater good of the freedom of the children of God. Hence, the need for a good spiritual director to guide and direct souls in this vocation of life.

Spiritual direction for consecrated religious must consider the specific charism and way of life of the directee's community. It should also be prepared to deal with several important stages of spiritual growth during preparation for consecration, such as deepening of vocation, examining the motive for entering religious life, and ensuring the proper degree of freedom to choose the life and sacrifices of a religious.

The director and directee might also need to consider and discuss the consecrated directee's "apostleship, fraternal life, and mission." They should also be prepared to discuss "questions concerning physical or moral solitude, failures, affective immaturity, sincere friendships, interior freedom in fidelity to obedience, peacefully assuming celibacy as a sign of Christ the Spouse for his Spouse which is the Church, etc."[71] Men and women religious have a distinct spousal relationship with the Lord. This deep commitment invites special consideration and attention by priests during the practice of spiritual direction.

Considerations for the laity include remembering the universal call to holiness and that they, too, are called to be prophetic witnesses for Christ. The laity are called to perfection, just like those in other vocations. Yet they are called to bring Christian values and ideals to the world and the temporal order in the areas of "social, family and professional engagement." The lay vocation is distinguished as "an evangelical leaven in the world and which operates within its proper sphere and in communion with the Church."[72] They live out their faith in the world, bringing the Gospel to family, public, and social life.

God gives the laity a special grace to help them reform these areas according to a

---

[71] Ibid., §119.

[72] Ibid., §122.

Christian spirit. Marriage is a specific vocation in which a man and woman come to realize the general vocation of holiness by entering into what *Gaudium et Spes* describes as an "intimate partnership of married life and love" [73] as a lifelong, exclusive, communion of persons of total and mutual self-giving and receiving. This covenant, as a sacrament, is an effective sign of grace that signifies and communicates the love between Christ and his Church. Besides conjugal love, the marriage realizes the vocation to holiness in the procreation and education of children, which forms a new communion of persons in the family. Marriage undoubtedly is a vocation to holiness that needs a specific spiritual direction.

Therefore, "the spiritual director should assist the lay faithful in their relationship with God (by making concrete their participation in the Holy Eucharist and prayer, in the examination of conscience in a manner that is in union with their lives) assisting in formation of conscience, support with the sanctification of the family, work social relationships, and taking

---

[73] Gaudium et Spes, §48, http://www.vatican.va/archive/hist_councils/ii_vatican_council/documents/vat-ii_cons_19651207_gaudium-et-spes_en.html

part in public life."[74] These human dimensions are orientated towards configuration of incarnational nature of Christ. "These various aspects of formation harmonize reciprocally to each other in view of ecclesial communion and mission."[75]

All three vocations require "a need to learn to listen" and assist each other by the development of human virtue cultivated in the light of faith, hope and charity. Hence, marriage, consecrated life and priesthood are three specific vocations in realizing the general vocation to the perfection of charity, and so the necessity of having and effective spiritual director to guide each according to his or her proper vocation.[76]

Role Play: A long-time practicing Catholic woman is now questioning her faith. She has been defending the church in the sexual abuse scandals until her nephew was devastated by her pastor. Now, she feels that she cannot trust any member of the clergy and can no longer pray. But something within her kept telling her

---

[74] Congregation for the Clergy, *The Priest, Minister of Divine Mercy*, §122.

[75] Ibid., §125.

[76] Ibid., §84.

to hold on to her faith and know that God exists beyond that dark side of the church. She still feels wounded and abandoned by God and the Church. She comes to you as a director for a way ahead.

What would *you* say to your directee?

VIII

Stages in Authentic Spiritual Direction

It is a respected opinion among experienced directors that sessions of spiritual direction should be as spontaneous and informal as possible to ensure that the directee feels comfortable and at ease without losing sight of the seriousness of the enterprise at hand. It is recommended that each session open with a brief shared prayer by both director and directee. It is always better for the director to ask the directee to lead in the prayer for the simple reason that the director may from the prayer already figure out more or less where the spirit is inviting him for help. However, if the directee is incapable, the director should take on that responsibility.

It is generally expected that a normal spiritual direction session should not exceed an hour and should not be less than an hour;

otherwise, it may result in the directee feeling cheated or that the director is not disposed. The opening minutes of the session may be spent in exchange of pleasantries especially on how things have been going with the directee, about home, family and work, but this should not be more than five minutes. It goes without saying that the rest of the hour should be engaged in real business at hand, that is, the spiritual growth of the directee, making sure that the conversation does not sidetrack into irrelevant topics. It is not advisable to keep written records of the directees nor tape any of the spiritual direction sessions. This is part of the mutually understood contract of confidentiality that is necessary between the director and directee.

Things to discuss at the first session include: personal data, previous religious experiences, personal relationship with God, relationship with neighbor, relationship with self and relation with nature. Direction on these four areas are important from the very onset because "unless the directee is really serious about prayer, ministry to others and self-discipline, the whole effort of spiritual direction will be in vain. Ordinarily, a director should not agree to give ongoing direction to a person who lacks seriousness of purpose about spiritual growth in the four relationships of love of God, neighbor, self and nature.[77]

In case there is not enough time in the first session to cover all the four relationships of love, the director would have achieved a good deal if he is able to get a fairly clear picture of the prayer life of the directee. The others, none-theless, should be addressed as soon as possible since all four relationships are closely inter-related and interdependent for the directee to come to a holistic spiritual growth.

During the first session, the emphasis should be on the positive elements of the directee's relationship with God. Sharing of past sins, failures and faults will be discussed during the later sessions. The director by emphasizing the positive will set the tone for the future relationship between him- or herself and the directee and show the directee the right attitude to maintain towards God.

The director will see that the directee does not take too many commitments as to lead to failure and discouragement. It is better to take such commitments bit by bit and thus gradually

---

[77] M. P. Chester, *An introduction to Spiritual Direction. A Psychological Approach to Directors and Directees.* (New York: Paulist Press, 2004), 34.

and successfully grow to higher and greater commitment. There is need for the directee and director to discuss about the directee's personal growth plan for the intervening time before the next meeting which will constitute the first thing to share at the meeting.

The goal of the spiritual director is to get the directee to grow in his or her relationship with God—to aim for closer union with the Divine Will. This involves using a tremendous amount of listening, theological knowledge and interpersonal skills. One of the most important qualities of a spiritual director is genuine warmth, including a real desire to help the directee. The director's relationship with God should be warm and loving. This will help the director be warm and affirming with the directee as well. Certainly, a close relationship with God means that a director will also be able to be more emotionally and spiritually intimate with the directee. Warmth is necessary for a number of reasons, mainly because it will help retain the directee/director relationship so that the desired goal can be reached through continuous sessions.

Warmth establishes a real connection between the directee and director. A spirit of love and affection will help build trust and intimacy. This strong connection will help the directee be more open and honest. The directee will believe that the director cares and will be more amenable to his or her guidance and questions. The director's warmth will help the directee "risk entrusting [him- or herself] to spiritual directors. ...Many do not know whether their thoughts, their feelings, their experiences are worth another person's time or are intelligible. They are afraid of being thought crazy or laughable. Or they are afraid that what they have to say may seem 'so ordinary,' 'so banal,' 'so common.' They need to sense the warmth of the director in order even to begin the process."[78]

Certainly, establishing this warmth will better ensure that progress is made, the direction sessions are fruitful and the direction able to continue to move forward. In time, establishing warmth helps establish trust and camaraderie between director and directee—making it more likely that the directee will be able to "go deep" and really examine and express his or her emotions about particular experiences. In turn, this will help the director discern which thoughts are from God and which are not.

---

[78] Barry and Connolly, *The Practice of Spiritual Direction*, 134.

Warmth is paramount and integral to not only retaining the directee, but to the directee's making real progress in holiness. Quite plainly, if the subsequent sessions of spiritual direction are mere formality, cold and stuffy, the directee is likely to abandon spiritual direction altogether for want of feeling loved, appreciated and respected as a child of God. Who wants to commit him- or herself to a process where he or she does not feel wanted and the atmosphere is consistently cold or confrontational?

Maintaining continuity is essential to the success of spiritual direction and to real progress being made by the directee. Burke and Bartunek sagely emphasize this point, time and time again, in their *Navigating the Interior Life* writing, "As with exercise, regularity is critical to develop spiritual momentum and strength. Brief bursts of spiritual fervor rarely result in the peace and fulfillment that Christ makes available for every pilgrim in the Faith."[79] Subsequent sessions need to soberly review the progress made by the directee to his or her goals set at the prior meeting. The directee's commitments need to be established within a fixed timeline.

---

[79] Burke and Bartunek, *Navigating the Interior Life*, 51.

Exploring the vital importance of warmth in subsequent sessions, Barry and Connolly reflect in their *Practice of Spiritual Direction*, "How does this 'surplus of warmth,' this love for people as they are, show itself in spiritual direction? It appears in three attitudes: commitment, effort to understand, and spontaneity."[80] As Barry and Connolly point out, warmth means loving the directee by means of a real commitment to help the directee grow in his or her relationship with the Trinity, seeking to actively listen to the directee, and by the director's likewise being true to him- or herself and warmly interacting with the directee to help the directee grow and progress.

If spiritual directors, receive their directees with warmth and love, they are more likely to retain them in spiritual direction and to see them advance in the love of God and neighbor by the grace of God.

Since warmth is required of a spiritual director at the initial encounter and throughout the subsequent meetings with a directee, both while in session and outside, it is important that spiritual directors have a naturally welcoming

---

[80] Barry and Connolly, *The Practice of Spiritual Direction*, 133.

disposition and that they genuinely care for people.

Being conscientious at one's personal interior life and having concerns for the general welfare of others in the sense of the society at large does not warrant a call for becoming a Spiritual Director. It is also important to note that warmth here does not include the cultural expression for embrace and cheek-kissing, nor does it include back rubbing, no matter how pure those gentle and loving expressions are. In fact, professional etiquette advises against these types of expression. And that is important to bear in mind. The Spiritual Director *is* a professional vocation although it is rarely, but not inappropriately, described as a career—just as being a priest is not deemed as a career but a vocation.

Barry & Connolly in "The Practice of Spiritual Direction" define the warmth characteristic required of a spiritual director as "love for people as they are."[81] This love "appears in three attitudes: commitment to help directees grow in union with God, to commit time, resources, and oneself to that end; effort to understand or to maintain a contemplative attitude toward directees, that is, to try to perceive how the directees experience God and life; and spontaneity or

---

[81] Ibid., 133.

being oneself, able to express one's own feelings, thoughts, and hopes (when expressing them will be helpful to directees) without which commitment and effort to understand will appear cold, impersonal, and stereotyped."[82]

Such warmth works for both director and directees in sustaining their relationship through the "gruesome" realities of feeling down (useless, ineffective, unworthy of one's time and effort), facing harsh comments from others who are at a disadvantage because of the changes in the directees, being vulnerable (having to expose the self to another person and asked to see and face one's own weakness) and falling prey to the human tendency to be judgmental, bored and easily distracted. Unconditioned love toward the directee helps the spiritual director in listening attentively and actively, which leads to knowing the directee more fully by under-standing his or her background, current situations, natural disposition and strengths. It also helps in generating empathy to understand the challenges that the directee has to face and overcome. These attitudes will consequently nurture trust and the feelings of being worthy and loved, which encourage the directee to persevere. Even more so, it brings the exper-ience of God, Who is Love, to the directee. When

---

[82] Ibid.

this is felt by the directee, there is no danger that he or she will revert.

Genuine warmth is also an indication that the directee greatly desires a stronger relationship with God. The directee's desire for God is an essential ingredient to successful spiritual direction. A director's recognition of this elicits positive feelings. "On the part of directors, the working alliance is an expression of the warmth for this other person that has been elicited by his or her sincere desire to know God better."[83] So, the two human persons in the relationship form a committed team to the goals of the "working alliance" and are more likely to continue to work towards those goals.

Boundaries are also an important consideration. Warmth does not mean a "physical, sexual or emotionally-dependent relationship."[84] Crossing this boundary does not include the directee's healthy affection for the director. It is common to have warm and appreciative feelings for someone who helps you. This ensures that the directee will trust that he or she can continue to be helped by the director during subsequent meetings.

---

[83] Ibid.

[84] Burke and Bartunek, *Navigating the Interior Life* (Kindle Locations 742-743).

The adage "they must know that you care before they care what you know" applies here. A directee is more likely to consider and take seriously the director's questions and knowledge if he or she believes that it comes from a place of love and genuine desire to help. The directee will continue to come back for future sessions because he or she senses the director's concern.

Spiritual directors should not be surprised by what a directee says because the director's disposition and mindset is more like a "lost and found" exercise. A director cannot come right out and ask, "What is your issue or problem!?" It is a director's responsibility to not interfere with the directee's open juncture with the Holy Spirit's guidance. Therefore, hearing outrageous, off-the-cuff comments should not lead a spiritual director to become judgmental or surprised by strong emotional or personal information from directee. Through warm questioning sessions, a director should try to lead a directee to discover his or her deep feelings associated with experiences of far-out events in life that needs answering.

Role Play:

Mathew has been married for five years to Ruth. The two of them have had four children over the years. Both are very good practicing Catholics, frequenting the sacraments. Just as with every family, they had minor family problem and invited Fr. Pat for family pastoral counseling. Fr. Pat did a fabulous job by putting them back in shape. Just to follow up with the direction, Fr. Pat kept visiting and calling the family. But Mathew could not understand the reason for this continual visit from Fr. Pat as they are done with their family problem. He kept showing this in so many ways. For instance, he stopped coming up to communion and started to avoid Fr. Pat at Church. He also stopped answering his phone calls. A year later, Ruth fell sick with cancer and was hospitalized for few days. Fr. Pat visited almost every day. Mathew often sits quietly in the room when Fr. Pat is speaking to his wife. Fr. Pat could not understand this unusual behavior of Mathew and came to you for direction.

What would *you* say to your directee?

IX

The Role of Psychology in Spiritual Direction

Since the early 80's there has been a near deluge of books and articles that explicitly incorporate clinical psychological methods into the practice of spiritual direction. [85] Other authors have gone beyond merely pointing out the relevance of psychology to spiritual direction. They have gone as far as suggesting the integration of the two disciplines.[86]

Man is a composite being with a corporeal, mortal body and a spiritual, immortal soul.

---

[85] Barry and Connolly, *The Practice of Spiritual Direction*; G. G. May, *Care of Mind/Care of Spirit: A Psychiatrist Explores Spiritual Direction* (San Francisco: HarperCollins, 1992).

[86] Len Sperry, *Transforming self and community: Revisioning Pastoral Counseling and Spiritual Direction*. (Collegeville: Liturgical Press, 2002).

Since spiritual direction primarily concerns man's relationship with God and secondarily with neighbor, spiritual direction is necessarily concerned with the whole of man and seeks the integration of all the powers of man's soul (intellect, will, and passions) by grace and transformation in the love of God. Psychology, then, plays a necessary role in spiritual direction, but spiritual direction cannot and must not be reduced to a counseling session or psychotherapy.

A spiritual director must have the humility to recognize his own limitations (in many cases he is not a qualified psychologist or psychiatrist). A certain degree of understanding of psychology is, however, necessary, particularly as it concerns topics such as the temperaments and the corresponding predominant vices and virtues, as well as how temperament can aid or hinder growth in prayer and resolute virtue. In a word, since the *whole* man encounters God in the sacraments, in prayer and in daily life, the spiritual director needs to have some grasp of human psychology.

The danger to avoid is this one: spiritual directors can quickly confuse psychology with spiritual direction and apply psychological principles to spiritual direction without adequate knowledge and reflection and thereby lose sight of the very purpose of spiritual direction: holiness.

If a spiritual director were to naively attempt to start psychoanalyzing the directee or do anything like clinically diagnose repressive neurosis, the director would fail to stay on target with the goal of spiritual direction and instead confound spiritual direction with mental health; this is clearly dangerous and all the more dangerous as many leading contemporary psychologists have abandoned Aristotelian philosophy and the truths of our Catholic faith.

Much of the psychology necessary for spiritual direction is acquired by the director through a healthy, integrated, mature personal life, which has known both the joys and sorrows ever-present in this passing life; a healthy, nurturing home life is of great benefit to the spiritual director, which allows the emotions to be rightly ordered to reason.

From a different perspective, consider the dark nights of St. John of the Cross, which the soul traverses in its pursuit of union with God. If the spiritual director is so naive that he does not recognize the melancholic temperament of his directee and likewise fails to understand what signs indicate that the soul is truly experiencing the dark nights, every melancholic the director directs will be in the dark nights.

This is clearly ludicrous. In a word, some knowledge of orthodox, solid psychology is of great benefit to the director, but we must be careful to stay right on track in spiritual direction, seeking to be the instrument of the Paraclete, that the directee might know and do God's will to arrive at the unending felicity of heaven.

In the mystery of the human person, it is problematic to try to separate the fostering of emotional growth from the personal experience of God. Spiritual experience is received in and for the totality of the human person. Psycho-therapy, on the other hand, goes deeper and is primarily focused on the emotional life in order to assist clients in healing past hurts and looking at and resolving unhealthy patterns in their lives. A good therapist will explore how clients are using their emotions and how their thoughts interact with their feelings.

It is pertinent to note that in spiritual direc-tion it is not unusual for emotional patterns or fears to be obstacles to growth in holiness, and these may need therapeutic attention that is beyond the director's scope of expertise. For instance, those suffering from severe anxiety or depression or from scrupulosity, a form of obsessive-compulsive disorder, would benefit from psychotherapy to reduce their distress and expose and heal the root cause of their problem. In that context, a working relationship between the spiritual director and the therapist, with the client's permission and cooperation, would be the best approach. Therefore, the purpose of psychology in spiritual direction will be to remove the emotional and psychological impediments to union with God and communion with others.

A spiritual director needs to be psychologically literate in order to listen to a directee's interior experiences. [87] This basic literacy will

---

[87] Considering someone who is going through despair and spiritual dryness at the same time, it is important to exercise the theological virtue of hope, trusting in God's goodness, the Divine Assistance of grace, and hoping in the ultimate good, eternal life. Spiritual dryness is distinct from despair because a soul experiencing aridity in prayer is not so much despairing as he or she is not sensibly experiencing the Divine Presence or the previously enjoyed consolations and good feelings. If, however, as can indeed be the case, the soul experiences despair and spiritual dryness simultaneously, it is important to first determine what is causing these feelings of despair. Are they distinct from the dryness? Moreover, is the spiritual aridity abiding and is the soul arriving at this spiritual dryness after having embarked upon Gospel living and an earnest attempt to live a sacramental life, growing in virtue

also help the director to recognize his own limitations regarding the use of more psychological techniques available to him. This basic literacy will help guard against the harm that can arise from projection and transference. Exceptions to the requirement of this psychological literacy occur with those rare persons who are so gifted by both nature and grace that they can compassionately read another's heart as Jesus did with the Samaritan woman at the well (Jn 4) and with Nicodemus, who came to him by night (Jn 3). The stories around the giftedness of the Curé of Ars and Brother André of Montreal exemplify this.

---

and rooting out vice? If so, it is quite possible that God is leading the soul into the dark night of the senses where God begins to communicate Himself to the soul, but because the soul is not yet prepared and purged, the divine communications are referred to as darkness. We might think of a man that sits in a dark room all day and is literally blinded when he emerges into the brilliance of the noonday sun. If the soul is entering into the dark night, it is of the greatest importance that the soul not turn back to its earlier ways of prayer but courageously and faithfully exercise what St. John of the Cross refers to as "anagogical acts," or acts of faith, hope and charity that dispose the person to the influx of God's transforming love and grace.

The dangers involved in indiscriminate application of psychology in spiritual direction can be a disaster in a certain sense for the directee. The director might neglect the activities of the Holy Spirit, Who is the principal director. How can the director be able to identify what is psychotic and what is genuine religious experience? A director must know what the human experience means in general before he can know what it means in any particular context.

While spiritual direction is not psychological counseling, then, it is helpful for directors to know something about behavior, cognition and emotions. Spiritual direction, unlike pastoral counselling, always happens in the context of prayer and spiritual intimacy. This is where intimate engagement happens, whereas in psychotherapy, the clinical distance is crucial to bringing about objectivity and healing. In spiritual direction, discernment is based upon the intimate engagement of two people walking into the presence of God in union with the Holy Spirit.

Spiritual direction is like others helping interaction. The more one knows about the person and the interpersonal the better one can relate to others in a helpful way. What is needed is a basic grasp of human psychodynamics and some familiarity with interpersonal skills. In the words of Thomas Hart, good spiritual directors are naturally self-reflective, and have a good grasp of their own psychic life. They know how to talk with people, how to listen emphatically and perceptively and how to express themselves clearly and appropriately. They pick up nonverbal as well as verbal communication. They can ask questions which prompt heuristic reflection, can give freedom and leave responsibility where it belongs and can help someone sort through a rambling report. They know how to clarify a confused message by checking out what they heard. They are at home in the world of feelings, their own and the other person's. They understand how to give a constructive feedback. They also know when what they are dealing with goes beyond their competence and they can refer it to someone better qualified.[88] These are some of the things sought in the kind of psychological formation envisaged for spiritual directors. Some people seem to be born with these qualities or to have acquired them very early in life. But training is needed too. Spiritual directors should also be familiar with personality development and

---

[88] Thomas Hart, *The Art of Christian Listening*, (New York: Paulist Press, 1980), 98.

psychopathology. There is clearly a developmental dimension of human life.

Man is body, mind and spirit. While the art of spiritual direction is primarily concerned with discerning God's will and deepening one's faith, this discernment takes place in the context of relationships. Both director and directee have a personal relationship with God as well as with each other. In addition, both people bring into the direction sessions their previous and current experiences of God and others. Both conscious and unconscious psychological factors will be at play in how they will interact and process the spiritual dimensions of their experiences, memories and thoughts. Because of this, a skilled spiritual director should have a basic grasp of human psychodynamics and some familiarity with interpersonal skills and be familiar with personality development and psychopathology.

According to dictionary.com, Psychology is "the science of the mind or of mental states and processes." The director's awareness of psychological principles can help him or her to recognize and point out to the directee when a certain approach toward God or an idea about God (either conscious or subconscious) is acting as a block to spiritual progress. The awareness of it and reference to such psychological ideas may be enough, but referral to a therapist or counselor might be an additional tool necessary. The director should not go beyond his or her competence.

The director should understand that he or she is not a psychologist or counselor; in a sense, spiritual direction supersedes psychology because God is not limited to what one perceives or has experienced—psychology is a science and its principles can only be applied to one's knowledge and experiences of the world. God's healing, knowledge and power is limitless. But it is important to understand that the haphazard or thoughtless application of psychology during spiritual direction can be quite dangerous.

Some of these dangers include:

Labeling: May lead to objectification of the person and "unnecessarily reduce the wonder of his or her reality." The psycho-pathology should not define the person and become the topic of discussions; it is curiosity about God's relationship that is the focus of the sessions.

Slowing of Spiritual Growth: When sessions become focused on psychological exploration, the subjective spiritual experiences are not discussed and the directee's relationship with God doesn't grow. "Mental and emotional concerns may kidnap the gentle spiritual attentiveness required of both director and directee."[89]

Director Becoming Healer: If the director is giving psychological advice, he or she becomes the healer, not God. In spiritual direction, God is the deity, not the director. God does the nurturing and liberating; the director and directee are "expressions of grace for each other."[90]

Neglecting of Primary Path to God: Self-understanding becomes the center of spiritual direction, rather than the deeper dimension of spirituality and one's experience and relationship to God.

The all-knowing, loving God is aware of our subconscious thoughts. That is why it's even more important to have a good spiritual director; he or she can serve as a very valuable guide to correctly discern what is of God and what is our own subconscious psychological neuroses or thoughts coming out in our ideas. A

---

[89] Ibid., 15.
[90] Ibid., 18.

good spiritual director will be able to know "what he or she doesn't know." In other words, he or she will be familiar enough with psychological ideas to know when a referral to a licensed mental health professional is in order.

The spiritual and the psychological can integrate together, and a good therapist will not say or do anything to undo the good spiritual work that is being done in spiritual direction. Ultimately, can God heal us of any spiritual or psychological dilemmas or challenges? Yes. But is that his will for us to simply be miraculously and suddenly healed? Not necessarily. God in his own way disposes us to accept that we might be healed slowly, bit by bit, as we take up our crosses and learn to deal with spiritual and psychological challenges.

God does not simply work for us but works with us, in us and definitely for us. That is the foundation of any spiritual journey—Prima Gratia, grace comes first but we need to cooperate with it. It's helpful to remember that spiritual direction is helping the other person discern how and what God is saying to him. The director has to be careful not to give advice, but to help the directee to determine God's will. In other words, humility is a key.

Role Play:

You oversee formation at a house of formation run by your international order. One of the seminarians comes to talk with you about a classmate of his named George. He says he is worried about the fact that the young man stays up late at night and often watches pornographic films. He also purchases pornographic pictures and magazines from the nearby store. He is in a questionable relationship with his fellow seminarian, Patrick, who comes to his room late in the night. His academic work is slipping, as is apparent from the way he seems unprepared for class discussions of assigned topics.

You call George in to talk with him. You tell him about the concern his classmate has expressed. George is quick to reassure you that his current interest in pornography is connected with his preparation of an article he is writing for the local diocesan newspaper. He says he has never tried to conceal his use of pornography for literary purposes and complains that other students ought to be mature enough to understand and accept his unobjectionable involvement in it and defensively attacks whoever must have reported him about his clean relationship with Patrick.

You explore with George what his interest in pornography means. Help him to open up to the Holy Spirit for discernment of his vocation to the Catholic Priesthood.

What would *you* say to your directee?

X

Signs of Growth in Discernment in the Ministry of Spiritual Direction

The central focus and the immediate goal of spiritual direction is growth in the life of union with God in Jesus Christ. The physical, emotional, moral, intellectual and relational life of the directee comes under reflection in Spiritual Direction, but they do so only in so far as these experiences express or improve the directee's life of union with God in faith and love through the Spirit of Jesus Christ the Divine Mercy Incarnate. The intellectual goal of spiritual direction is transformation of consciousness. We gradually come to think about God, other persons, the whole cosmos and ourselves as they appear in the light of revelation. In other words, spiritual direction works to bring the director and directee to think of all things as God thinks of them.

The ultimate spiritual goal of spiritual direction is the fullness of union with God in Jesus Christ. The goal of spiritual direction is the same as the goal of Christian life itself; to become ever more completely transformed into the likeness of Christ by the action of the Holy Spirit upon our body, soul and spirit. The grace of God is the original source and means to the goal of Christian life. This divine grace provides the seed and the growth of the gift and virtue of discernment of thoughts and action.

To grow in discernment within the ministry of spiritual direction, it is necessary for the direction itself to follow a process leading to

- prayer,
- humility,
- detachment from preferences,
- a strengthening of listening ability,
- a study of the life and teaching of the saints,
- knowledge of the teaching of the Church,
- careful examination of personal interior inclinations,
- an ability to change and freedom of heart.

This process will guarantee a sure part toward growth in discernment in spiritual life. The directee will develop an attitude of submission and willing abandonment until transformed by charity into a true child of God. The directee will gradually grow in self-knowledge as the closer we get to God, the more we see our true selves before the God who loves us unconditionally. It is the knowledge of what we are and of what we are worth that will permit us to take before God the attitude of truth that is required.

Through the ministry of spiritual direction, the directee will grow in effective prayer life, the awareness of God's presence in his or her daily life. The growth will also include openness to the will of God regarding vocation or mission and the constant desire towards the life of holiness. The important point is that the directee-director relationship with the Lord is always growing and maturing, so both can recognize his voice as they travel with Him along the path to Heaven.

Some have mistakenly defined spiritual discernment as a God-given awareness of evil, but spiritual discernment has to do with wisdom and the ability to distinguish truth from error or good spiritual presences, not necessarily the ability to tell if a demon is in the room. While some people may possess this capability, it is not the biblical meaning of discernment. For a directee, spiritual discernment ultimately has to do with wisdom and the ability to distinguish truth from error and growing in the knowledge and love of God.

The sacred scriptures say that Jesus Christ is "wisdom from God" (1 Cor 1:30). Therefore, wisdom, or spiritual discernment, [91] is something that comes from knowing Jesus Christ. The world's way of getting wisdom is different from God's way. The learned of the world gain knowledge and apply reason to knowledge to solve problems, construct buildings and create philosophies. But God does not make the knowledge of Himself available by those means. We learn to be spiritually discerning by knowing Him.

For the spiritual director to aid the directee in assessing his or her relationship with God and

---

[91] "Discernment is faithful living and listening to God's love and direction so that we can fulfill our individual calling and shared mission," writes Henri Nouwen in *Discernment: Reading the Signs of Daily Life* (Harper One 2013). He adds that "Living a spiritually mature life requires listening to God's voice within and among us. To discern means first of all to listen to God, to pay attention to God's active presence, and to obey God's prompting, direction, leadings, and guidance. Discernment of spirits is a lifelong task. I can see no other way for discernment than to be committed to a life of unceasing prayer and contemplation, a life of deep communion with the Spirit of God."

neighbor, it is imperative to begin with a firm understanding of discernment and the accompanying signs that reveal that there is growth in discernment. *The Priest, Minister of Divine Mercy* states, "It is easier to discern the *work of the Holy Spirit* in the life of each individual with the assistance of spiritual direction conducted in the light of a lived faith. This inevitably leads to prayer, humility, sacrifice, the ordinary life of Nazareth, service, and hope."[92] This list of the signs of growth in discernment from the Congregation for the Clergy is remarkably complete in its conciseness, but might be expounded to include a desire to serve God and neighbor, patience in bearing one's crosses, Gospel poverty and detachment proper to one's state in life, embracing suffering for love of God and others, despising sin and fleeing from its occasions, recognizing the rejection by the world that comes with following Christ, being faithful to a rich interior life, developing a rightly formed conscience rooted in humility and obedience, and an unquenchable thirst for the Truth that is God.

Barry, therefore, sagely concludes in *Spiritual Direction and the Encounter with*

---

[92] Congregation for the Clergy, *The Priest, Minister of Divine Mercy*, §98.

God, "Thus, the best criterion by which to discern God's action in one's life is the sense of a developing inner and outer harmony, a growing sense of one's own self as distinct from and independent of, yet related to, important other people, one's world, one's God."[93]

By contrast, *The Priest, Minister of Divine Mercy* also identifies that the destructive fruits of evil are "accompanied by pride, independence, sadness, discouragement, jealousy, confusion, hatred, deception, disdain of others, and selfish preferences."[94] These signs, too, are important for the spiritual director to be vigilant about! There are also signs of a religious or priestly vocation, as well as special discernment needed in the difficult personal and community situations encountered in this earthly life.

Fr. Dubay offers a further critically important point in making good discernment, namely that discernment of growth must necessarily not be based on feelings. Dubay writes in *Seeking Spiritual Direction*, "Perhaps the most common mistake people make in assessing their progress is to judge it by the standard of feeling ... While Scripture surely speaks often of genuine exper-

---

[93] Barry, *Spiritual Direction and the Encounter with God*, 81-82.

[94] Congregation for the Clergy, *The Priest, Minister of Divine Mercy*, §99.

iences of God, nowhere does it present feelings as decisive criteria of progress or dry 'emptiness' as an indication of fault or mediocrity. Yet, this is how most people look at the matter. What we do find over and over in God's word is the message that growth is shown in a concrete, down-to-earth identification of our wills with the divine will."[95]

As *The Priest: Minister of the Divine Mercy* points out, "it is not possible to formulate strict norms about discernment. However, the saints and the spiritual masters continually refer to certain constants or to signs of the actions of the Spirit..." (§100) Based on the experiences of these holy people, we can expect signs ("certain constants") to be present in ourselves and in our directees as a result of fruitful spiritual direction.

Perhaps the very first sign of growth in discernment as a result of spiritual direction is the restless feeling of being unfulfilled. This is when we start to know that "there is *something* God is calling me for," even as we are unsure what it is. As their spiritual direction progresses, they will gradually discover their true vocation and find relief in taking the steps toward its fulfillment. Some people may experience it differently. They may (sort of)

---

[95] Dubay, *Seeking Spiritual Direction*, 268-269.

know what God is calling them for, but they were not one hundred percent sure of it. In their case the sign of growth is found in the assurance for their call, which manifest in peace and a joyful acceptance that flows from their heart out to their outer appearance.

Whether you start with restlessness or you just need the confirmation of the Spirit, eventually the Spirit of Truth will bring joy and you will be happy with who you are and be at peace with all the happenings in your lives. Fr. Barry describes this as "live in the now with a relative lack of ambivalence and fear, attuned to the Presence of God... You know that you are at the right place at the right time... be extraordinarily free, happy, and fulfilled even the midst of a world of sorrow and pain."[96]

The further one grows in the discernment of the Spirit, the person will experience some "purging" by means of being more sensitive to his or her own conscience or what Fr. Dubay calls the "delicacy of conscience."[97] The "voice" in one's conscience is the guidance of the indwelling Spirit. The more we are attuned to it, the more we become "identified" with Godly attributes: holy, loving, just, merciful, etc. We

[96] Barry, *Spiritual Direction and Encounter with God*, 78.

[97] Dubay, *Seeking Spiritual Direction*, 274.

feel sorrow and remorse at the slightest offense against the sanctity of God and our heart will not rest until we have been absolved from our sin and renew our relationship with God. This sensitivity to the guidance of the Holy Spirit inevitably makes us more and more obedient to God, which will manifest in our pulling away from any selfish action and motivation, away from all kinds of vanity, and increase our love for truth, for the Church, for people who have yet to know God or who have yet learned the fullness of God's love for the world. We become more compassionate toward these people and become more concerned for the work of the Evangelization.

As we continue to grow in perfection, we also become less worried and more dependent on God. "Perfect love casts out fear" (1 Jn 4:18) When we live in union with God, Who is the Perfect Love, we fear nothing, we may have some concerns about certain things in this world, but we are not worried, for we know that God is in charge. All we need to do is being in contemplative prayer as we breath in and breath out. We pray without ceasing as if everything depends on us, but we know confidently that everything depends on God, and thus we do what we can do according to His call and leave everything else to God.

Fr. Dominic Anaeto

To understand spiritual direction as a ministry of faith, a life of prayer is a requisite to "help us to deepen our contact with the promptings of the spirit and enable us to listen more and more as Christ listened to the God he called Abba, Father."[98] Contemplative prayer develops the necessary skill set for active listening. When we offer a sympathetic and caring disposition to another, it deepens our connection to the mystery of divine will in wisdom, unity and hope. Spiritual conversion is not manifested by rational analysis but by a living and cooperative relationship with God. This intimate connection with divine love is developed by true knowledge of Christ obtained by prayer and discernment thereby manifesting in signs or acts of moral and ethical responsibility, charity and mercy.

That being said, it is a forgone conclusion that the study of theology embraces the mystery of Christianity in a systematic response to the reality of meaning of human life in relationship to the incarnate Word. The nature of divine love in God is integrated in Man as the centerpiece of creation. Therefore, spiritual direction is a communion, so to speak, in the "created good"

---

[98] John Navone, S.J., *Self-giving and Sharing. The Trinity and Human Fulfillment* (Collegeville, MN: The Liturgical Press, 1989), 36.

which reforms the lives of those who are yearning to abide in God's goodness.

By way of interrelating theological and philosophical aspects of the Catholic Church into spiritual analysis initiatives, spiritual direction draws from both the rational and revelatory elements in verbal exchange thereby anchoring the salvific plan of redemption to the theology of the body in the concrete, that is, to eschatological man, which brings about personal fruition, a renewed state of fruitfulness and recovery, and a shaping of man into the likeness of the Triune family. "Henceforth we come to know the triune God in our interpersonal, interdependent, and loving fellowship by a maturity through the deepening of our relationships in the triune community through which we are nurtured and nurture one another freely, cooperatively, and peacefully."[99]

Thereafter, the ongoing process of discernment is fostered best by quieting our inner dialogue and connecting our efforts to a contemplative attitude that opens us up to the dimensions of mission and ministry. This interior conversion responds to Jesus's preaching that "no one [should] pour new wine into old wineskins. Otherwise, the wine will burst the skins, and both the wine and the wineskins will

---

[99] Ibid.

be ruined. No, they pour new wine into new wineskins." Jesus is telling us to consider the theological significance in daily life by unmasking self-deception and self-centered-ness in becoming a new person [disciple] in Christ.

Signs of resistance are exceedingly impor-tant for us to be aware of as directors that we might be vigilant for them in the directee. After all, resistances to God are indicative that the directee is struggling, and while signs of the spiritual battle can be positive, as Barry and Connolly reflect, they must also be properly used as springboards that open the directee to the divine encounter.

In other words, the resistances must not become roadblocks or cause the directee to abandon the spiritual life altogether. The director is invited to help the directee understand the resistances he or she places between him or her and God and neighbor and to then respond freely with an abundance of charity and in a mature manner. Barry and Connolly's mention of sleep as resistance.[100]

---

[100]Those resistances have great consequences on the relationship between the directee and God. The enemy comes to steal the directee's tenacity for the things of God. Suddenly the directee's prayer life seems stalled. The directee's commitment is tested

Certainly, in religious life, and in all walks of life, we get tired and can fall asleep before the Lord. The Little Flower speaks of this eloquently, noting that the Divine Child knows that we are tired. Frequent sleep, however, during prayer can likewise be a sign of resistance to that loving conversation with God. In that circumstance, the directee prefers to sleep rather than to apply him- or herself assiduously to prayer and to be attentive to God's voice.

The Practice of Spiritual Direction nuances this correctly, "[C]ontinued conversation with Jesus meant a radical departure from her [the

---

and can't seem to push through. He or she feel as though just going through the motions. The enemy bombards the mind with various thoughts and ongoing temptation in order to rob peace. The mind becomes irritated and exhausted. The enemy does all that he can to bring mental fatigue. As the enemy attacks the life of a directee, he or she begins to give reasons to give up on the very thing that God called them to, as a result of holding on to those resistances the enemy takes over the mind of the directee. The enemy releases confusion, shame, intimidation and a variety of vile schemes to create a cloud of uncertainty for the directee. For the directee to recover back to faith, he or she must pray at all times in the Spirit and seek help from the Blessed Mother.

directee's] past life. Before this abyss the only solution was to avoid looking [by rather sleeping]." This gets to the heart of the matter, which is that resistance, in whatever form, is really an attempt to be free from God and neighbor, rather than to be free *for* them. In this sense, we can put up barriers to avoid doing the work we really need to do, going out of ourselves in self-less, generous, boundless love to God and to one another.

Spiritual development peels experiential knowledge back to a higher order of knowing. Therefore, man does not do as he wills [by rational analysis only] but as he ought because he is nourished by prayer and divine truth [knowledge]. Man's thirst for truth is most realized by the promptings of the Holy Spirit and examinations of conscience.

Discernment will mold a person's person-hood to the understanding of theological under-standing and the appreciation of spiritual direction as a true nature of "loving thyself," thereby abiding in the Pascal mystery as the authentic cause and effect in humanity. This awakening into the realm of holiness prepares us to relate to our experiential circumstances and rationales which will move us toward or away from God if one so chooses.

Spiritual direction is the chariot that encircles the heart of Christ as we relate to one another. Our armor is manifested by the interaction of divine knowledge and justice in the concrete, validating the spirit of intimacy to "works that concerns an ongoing and gradual process of divinization that draws us into a deeper participation in the eternal celebration of love within the Godhead." [101] Spiritual direction is a ministry of faith seeking to understand freely the re-creative presence of God that hovers over and revives the primal forces within us.

Therefore, solitude, charity, prayer and freeness are the primary elements that helps us become ourselves in faith. As we move away from material attachment and into the fullness of life, the glory of God becomes clearer and dearer to our conversion process. Spiritual direction is a ministry that helps people to open up to themselves and open their hearts to the goodness of God himself. We find that in solitude an indispensable invitation is made by the Holy Spirit as both Father and friend growing into a precious one to one relationship that precedes life itself. These elements of

---

[101] **Dennis J.** Billy, C.Ss.R., "Spiritual Direction as Faith Seeking Understanding," *Seminary Journal* 19, no. 1 (2013), 28.

conversion harness body and spirit as one interrelational stirrup that dwells in the human soul. In other words, solitude, charity and prayer manifests a "tranquility of order" as Augustine of Hippo refers to it, possesses personal, communal and transcendent dimensions."[102]

Spiritual direction makes faith a more comprehensible application of the Gospel as "the living Word of God." Therefore, the economy of faith's mission is to develop an interpersonal relationship with oneself by seeking to understand God himself through "the Church as the actual living Word of God." The ministerial aspect of this relationship is when one evangelizes the faith outside of themselves for others in a meaningful way. As the manifold of life unfolds and the wisdom acquired from spiritual direction deepens, it collaborates with others as a personal touch. The benefit that comes out of spiritual wisdom is that our responses to circumstances and challenges that surprisingly prop up expectantly do not deter us from the pursuit of perfection.

All in all, spiritual direction is a process that cultivates our brokenness into new wineskins of virtue. Spiritual direction naturally shapes one in the "likeness and image" of God as "various

---

[102] Ibid.

dimensions of our human makeup: physical, emotional, intellectual, social and spiritual. With the help of our director, we try to identify which dimensions are neglected in prayer and take appropriate steps to achieve a proper balance in our lives."[103]

Our longing for holiness is a natural response to God's calling his flock [the Church] back home. Spiritual direction, prayer, introspection, charitable acts and the causation of the virtues transcends unity to the Trinitarian mystery by divine truth and justice in the Catholic Church. We share in holiness by the will of God. Spiritual direction is the "app" befitting man to the image and likeness of his Creator in both ministry and mission. Spiritual direction "teaches us to listen to the movement of the Spirit in our hearts and to respond accordingly, spiritual direction initiates us into the ways of wisdom. It does so by helping us view the world with eyes of compassion and with a sense of God's intense longing to dwell in our hearts."[104]

Spiritual direction is a friendship around spiritual matters which is mutual in love but single-directional in its focus upon the spiritual walk of one of the parties. As spiritual directors, we are the one who listens, paying attention for

---

[103] Ibid.
[104] Ibid.

the work of God in that person's life, and then we point to it.

Spiritual Direction helps us to step back from our busy life and contemplate how God is present to us and what God is saying to us. It makes us ever mindful in joy, sorrow, success and failure of the evidences of grace that we might otherwise overlook or take for granted. True knowledge of God involves an experience with the divine mystery, not simply knowledge about it. Such experiential knowledge does not come through rational analysis, but from a living relationship with God that is nourished by prayer.

We know that in spiritual direction, we try to help the person understand what happened when he or she received the good news, and what the good news means in his or her life now. Spiritual direction is not an attempt to find faith or create faith; it is an attempt to understand faith. Spiritual direction is faith seeking understanding. But it is faith seeking understanding in the most specific and personal sense. Spiritual direction is not jawing about theology. It is not a discussion about a theological object of faith. It is an intense search in a specific person's life for the Living Subject of faith already at work—looking for that work, pointing to that work so that the directee can participate in God's work, so that he or she can live in active covenant with God in everyday life.

The theological virtue of faith is an utter and sheer gift to us by the good God. The author to the letter to the Hebrews writes of faith as the "assurance of things hoped for, the conviction of things not seen" (Heb 11:1). Faith, however, must be formed by charity, which is to say carried out in concrete actions towards both God and neighbor. It is also important to maintain that while theological faith is supernatural, that is it is *beyond* what man could know without God's self-revelation, nothing that pertains to faith is *contrary* to reason. Consequently, man is called by His Creator to seek to know Him ever more perfectly that He might love God more selflessly and heroically.

Expressed differently, man is called to not simply know something about God, made certain by faith, but to enter into a relationship with the Trinity by which the creature experiences the love of the Creator in the mystery of the divine encounter, made perfect in the beatific vision. Even in this life, man is called to commune with God in love, which is sustained by the life-giving sacraments and fostered in prayer. Again, however, it is critical to repeat that this life of faith is formed by charity.

Pondered from yet another angle, it is helpful to recall that Christ Jesus is Truth. We creatures share in the Truth that is God when we come to know things as they really and truly are, first and foremost God Himself. We can, however, have a difficult time arriving at the truth when confronted with a quasi-infinite number of choices in this life. In order to enter the divine encounter with God Who is Truth, spiritual direction can be of the greatest advantage.

In an intriguing article by Fr. Dennis Billy, "Spiritual Direction as Faith Seeking Understanding," Billy writes, "Spiritual direction seeks to assist us in confronting ourselves and opening our hearts to God. It does so by gently helping us to recognize and then listen to the visit of the Spirit manifested in the nitty-gritty circumstances of our lives. More often than not, that voice, as the experience of the prophet Elijah reminds us, is found not in the tumultuous whirlwinds, earthquakes and fires about us, but in the still, small whispering sound that can only be heard in the solitude of our hearts."[105] Spiritual direction, thus, invites the directee to open his or her heart to the divine

---

[105] Ibid., 28.

that God might transform the directee in His infinite love and allow him or her to participate more fully in the divine life. Accordingly, spiritual direction, understood as *fides quarens intellectum*, seeks to identify and prayerfully discern the signs of God's activity in the directee's life in order to know and do God's Will.

Billy succinctly states, "The ministry of spiritual direction is an important arena where the acquisition of spiritual wisdom occurs."[106] Spiritual direction is of indescribable assistance in allowing the faith we profess to be lived joyfully, courageously, willingly, spontan-eously throughout all of life's moments, as we await the unending beatitude of heaven where what we now believe by faith we shall then behold by the light of glory.

St. Anselm had a sort of motto that sums up his life and teaching. In Latin, the famous motto is *fides quarens intellectum*. Which literally means "faith seeking understanding." It means that faith comes before understanding. We don't have to understand God in His entirety in order to have faith. Faith comes first, then it leads us to deeper understanding. We see this so clearly in the Easter season. When Mary Magdalene &

---

[106] Ibid., 30.

Peter & John went to the tomb and found it empty, they certainly did not understand everything that had happened. But, the Scriptures tell us that they "saw and believed" (John 20:8). Their lack of understanding didn't keep them from having faith. Rather, they began with faith, which led them to greater understanding at Pentecost and in the days and weeks that came after.

There is a strong connection between St Anselm's dictum or "motto" with spiritual direction ministry as faith seeking understanding. Through the faith of the directee in spiritual direction, he or she experiences a deeper understanding of the mysteries of God and the desire for holiness. Spiritual direction is not an attempt to find faith or create faith; it is an attempt to understand faith. Spiritual direction is faith-seeking understanding in essence. But it is faith-seeking understanding in the most specific and personal sense. Spiritual direction is not about theological dialogue in certain sense. It is not a discussion about a theological object of faith. It is an intense specific search in a directee's life for the living experience of faith already at work and looking for that work, pointing to that work so that the directee can participate in God's work, so that he or she can live in active covenant with God in everyday life. Through conversation and reflection, the directee becomes more attuned to God's Presence in his or her life and can respond more fully to God in every way.

In spiritual direction, the director helps the directee become more aware of and responsive to the real Presence of God, both in those activities called "religious" and in the ordinary and routine circumstances of daily life. While there is nothing that is inappropriate for a directee to bring to the spiritual direction conversation, anything discussed will always be discussed from the perspective of relationship with God. This is the unique focus of spiritual direction, and one of the main differences between direction and psychotherapy, or other forms of counseling. As our relationship with God is ongoing, so is spiritual direction ongoing.

The ministry of spiritual direction begins from where you are in your quest to live the Gospel message of Jesus Christ through your Christian faith. For someone just beginning the spiritual journey, spiritual direction offers insight and reflection into the fundamentals of committed prayer and what it means to live a sacramental and communal life of faith. For those that are more advanced, spiritual direc-tion focuses on a deepening life of prayer and a more serious discernment of one's gifts in vocation to God and His Church.

The religious experience is not isolated, nor does it consist of extraordinary events. It is what happens in an ongoing relationship between the person and God. Most often this is a relationship that is experienced in prayer. God is leading the person to deeper faith and more generous service. The spiritual director asks not just "what is happening?" but "what is moving forward in the life of the directee?" Ultimately, the Holy Spirit who is the "spiritual director" will lead the directee through faith and the understanding of the will of God.

As we understand from the books of the OT, (Jeremiah 10:23), "The way of man is not in himself; It is not in man who walks to direct his own steps". You need to find and study a source of spiritual direction and guidance from someone who really knows the answers. (Isaiah 55:8-9) People alone cannot provide this spiritual guidance. Many learned men do not even attempt to provide answers for the meaning and purpose of life and other serious spiritual questions. If they do try, they cannot prove their answers are right or wrong, and they often contradict one another. Therefore, spiritual direction with the goal of helping us become ourselves in our faith, helps us to talk to

God, to listen to him and to engage in an ongoing process of discernment that ultimately leads to deeper intimacy with Him.

Obstacles to a valid assessment is an inadequate grasp of discernment itself. Hence the need to know the signs of growth is discernment in spiritual direction. The signs are God-centeredness, an undivided heart, service to others, entering by the hard road, pilgrim frugality, suffering with love, hatred for sin, rejection by the world, fidelity to contemplative prayer, absence of egocentricism, delicacy of conscience, watching, obedience, humility, speech, a reflecting mirror, holy dissatisfaction, and love for truth and love for the church. [107] Therefore, the spiritual director in aiding his directee to discerning a specific vocation should make sure that it understand that the choice and living out of the various vocations should be primarily motivated out of a deep and profound love of God and neighbor and that all these vocations are paths to deeper communion with God.

Any other kind of motivation such as desire for fame and security or fear of marriage or members of the opposite gender should be purified toward seeking the kingdom of God first and foremost. Thus, it becomes incumbent

---

[107] Dubay, *Seeking Spiritual Direction*, 267-278.

on the director to encourage the directee to first seek purity of heart in the general call to holiness through living the sacramental life and living a virtuous life in union with Christ and with true devotion to Mary. Love as the primary motivation will be key in the directee's discernment of his or her vocation.

Discernment should not be reduced to an objective, cold analysis of what God is calling one to follow in the realization of the call to holiness. Such an approach of reducing discernment to human reasoning would be neglecting the most important element of discernment, which is the prayerful consideration of which state of life one can best love God and neighbor, done in God's loving presence. A certain purity of heart through prayer and graced Christian living is a necessary condition for the directed to be enlightened by God's light in asking for and making a good choice of his or her vocation.

If spiritual direction is progressing as it should, certain fruits should begin to become apparent. As well as growing in holiness and love of God and others, the directee should be growing in his or her ability to discern God's will. If this is taking place, there will be signs.

The directee will become more aware of attachments to non-spiritual things and seek to detach from them. He or she will "be filled with the utter fullness of Triune beauty." [108] This growing satisfaction with spiritual things may manifest itself in an outpouring of charitable works, both spiritual and physical.

As the relationship between the director and directee grows, the directee will gain an increased awareness of his or her own proclivities and inclinations. He or she will be better able to identify the ways in which God is speaking to him or her. The director has acted as a third party, a neutral observer, if you will, and prompted the directee to consider things in a new light—the light of Christ's truth and love.

Old sins may be set aside and become less frequent as the directee becomes a new creation, gaining a level of heroic virtue.[109] The directee may notice that the Holy Spirit's wisdom and guidance is sought more and more as he or she gives up his or her own preferences, is open to being led by God and does His will first.

Another sign that the directee is growing in discernment is if he or she is rejected by the world.[110] As Christ's message and truths become one's guiding principle, the message of the world is rejected, and the world in turn rejects the soul. Those who are not led by the Spirit "are

---

[108] Dubay, *Seeking Spiritual Direction*, 46.

[109] Ibid., 47.

[110] Ibid., 273.

of the world, and so they speak the language of the world and the world listens to them" (1 Jn 4:5). If the directee is speaking out and witnessing to Gospel truths, people who judge all things according to this world will likely begin to hate and attack him or her.

A certain peacefulness and feeling of being "in tune" with God and the world around oneself is apparent when one is aware of and doing God's will. This is the opposite of living in fear and primarily concerning oneself with one's own needs rather than the needs of others. Barry describes this as knowing that "you are in the right place at the right time."[111]

Additional signs of growing in discernment in spiritual direction include God-centeredness, an undivided heart, suffering with love, hatred for sin, fidelity to contemplative prayer, absence of egocentricism, delicacy of conscience, watching, obedience, humility, speech, a reflecting mirror, holy dissatisfaction, love for truth and love for the church.

In essence, the directee grows more aware of God's love and sees God in all things and in all people. He or she desires God's will and places God first in all things, producing interior peace

[111] Barry, *Spiritual Direction and the Encounter with God*, 78.

and acceptance of others. People and events are as God wills it, and the directee humbly accepts what he or she can or cannot do to change. The directee sees him- or herself clearly in relation to God and others (humility). A very real and strong growth in love for God overflows into thoughts and deeds centered around doing only the good, abhorring the tiniest sin, and increasingly desiring union with God.

Discernment in the ministry of spiritual direction requires a tranquil mind and heart with love for the Church. [112] Harmony is a gift of the Holy Spirit that "leads to prayer, humility, and sacrifice, the ordinary life of Nazareth, service, and hope" to the paschal joy in the Spirit. Those areas in life like contemplation, and pursuit of perfection, fraternal life and mission are piece and part to the path of vocational treasures. God-centeredness, an undivided heart and serving others are the fruitful signs that point to spiritual discernment.

Spiritual discernment cannot be formulated into strict norms because people are different and so are those areas (circumstances, time, and environment) which can add or subtract to one's preferred movement of choice in the pursuit of

---

[112] Congregation for the Clergy, *The Priest, Minister of Divine Mercy*, §98-100.

holiness. The best way to serve God and one brothers and sisters is to study the obedient lives of the saints. They demonstrated the necessities of discernment by "detachment from preferences, study of the teachings of the Church, careful examination of personal interior inclinations and the ability to change."[113]

Discernment must also be vigilant on how fear can cause or distort one's attitudes and motives in spiritual direction into defensive thinking and acting. Therefore, rather than cultivating a humble disposition, fear can cause one to evade moral and ethical responsibilities which are used to govern the sense of the common good of society with an undivided heart. Discernment therefore displaces fear because it controls one's destiny by putting his or her life in the palm of God's hand. Intellectual and emotional development "will not guarantee us security or pleasure or happiness or comfort; but discernment will give us what is more worth

---

[113]Just the process of discernment can help make someone more peaceful and in tune with God. Growth through spiritual direction should really produce an interior transformation of the heart. The fruit of this interior work can be observed by the director in the directee's actions, words and nonverbal communication.

having, a slow, gradual realization of the goodness of the world and of living in it."[114]

Discernment describes "feelings" not as a governing body to spiritual perfection but as a hatred of sin, a welcomed rejection from others, and humility rapt in fidelity to contemplative prayer as an internal gift that grasps and leads to the heart of reality "through a disciplined attention to our experience."[115] In other words, we attune our motives and feelings to the Holy Spirit who blows where ever it pleases. Therefore, we joyfully follow in Christ's footsteps as a humble servant by abiding in the actions of "good spirit"[116] both in "purpose and method," [117] which satisfies "the rule for the discernment of spirits"[118] in light of reason for personal growth and in ministry.

Another rule for the discernment of spirits is the endeavor to purify one's soul from sin, seeking to increase in the service of God seeking greater perfection by "removing all obstacles so that the soul goes forward in doing good."[119] It's

---

[114] Barry, *Spiritual Direction and the Encounter with God*, 75.
   [115] Ibid., 76.
   [116] Ibid., 77.
   [117] Ibid., 77.
   [118] Ibid., 76.
   [119] Ibid., 78.

interesting to note that every time I attend Mass my "character is discernible in the mental or moral attitude in which when it comes upon me, I feel most deeply and intensely active and alive. There is a voice inside which speaks and says: this is the real me."[120]

Examination of conscience is in order to adjust one's action in the present environment with the one action of God. As St. Ignatius describes, discernment is an exercise of prayer, walking with the Lord which is contemplative in the concrete. Discernment co-determines the future by acclimating every moment of every day to God's will.

Communal discernment adapts to the one action of God to "enable groups of ordinary people to trust one another enough to believe in their power to make society, or some part of it, more amenable to Gospel values." [121] "The general purpose of spiritual direction is identical with that of the whole economy of salvation, aiding the directee to love God with the whole heart, soul, and mind, and the neighbor as oneself." [122] Discernment "avoids making little gods of our needs and prefer-

[120] Ibid., 82.
[121] Ibid., 86.
[122] Dubay, *Seeking Spiritual Direction*, 46.

ences."[123] Discernment and spiritual direction go hand in hand because it enables the directee and director to be led by the primary director, the Holy Spirit.

Role Play:

Monica is married to Frank for five years now. Each year as the Holy season of lent approaches, they will always have serious family problem. The hub of the matter is always around the form their Lenten abstinence will take. Monica will always insist that Lent is a time to be pure before the Lord and not a time of love making, but Frank maintains the stand that love making is part and parcel of their spousal relationship and should not be limited to any season.

As the Lenten season is drawing near, Monica comes to you presenting the difficulty she is having in her marriage for you to help her talk to the husband to educate his sexual emotions only during that Holy Season of fasting and abstinence.

What would *you* say to your directee?

---

[123] Ibid., 46.

XI

Resistance and Signs of Resistance in Spiritual Direction

Man is created by God a free, rational creature, and man freely chooses his eternal destiny, the unending felicity of heaven and the direct vision or God **or** the unending pain of loss and sense of hell in the company of Satan and the fallen angels. Spiritual direction, squarely concerned with man's relationship with God and neighbor, is consequentially rooted in the natural freedom of the directee, which certainly includes both his or her freedom to choose a director and to either put into practice or fail to practice the counsel received in spiritual direction.

In other words, spiritual direction is utterly alien to coercion of any kind, but rather has the goal of helping the directee develop a mature, integrated freedom that places him or her in ever growing communion with the Trinity and neighbor. *The Priest, Minister of Divine Mercy* very beautifully summarizes, "It is the task of the spiritual director to assist the individual to choose and to choose responsibly that which he must do in the sight of God, with Christian maturity."[124]

There are, however, a few critical corresponding facts that must be born in mind and which in fact flow from the directee's freedom. In the first place, the directee ought not to flippantly switch from director to director in an attempt to have his own self-will placated and affirmed; this is very dangerous and can only be overcome by the directee's being reminded that the primary director in spiritual direction is the Holy Ghost Himself and the human director is His instrument. Expressed differently, the directee ought to approach spiritual direction with a spirit of *docility* and *humility*. *The Priest, Minister of Divine Mercy* goes so far as to teach that the very "authenticity of the spiritual life will be seen by the harmony that exists between the counsels that have been sought and received, and a life that is lived in practical

[124] Congregation for the Clergy, *The Priest, Minister of Divine Mercy*, §109.

coherence to these."[125] The second corresponding truth to the centrality of freedom in spiritual
direction is that the directee cannot and must
not place blame on the director for the directee's
actions, but instead recall that he or she freely
chose to follow the direction received or to
disregard it.

Considering contemporary confusion concerning the notion of freedom, it is imperative to
reaffirm that authentic freedom is not so much
freedom *from* something, but rather freedom *for* God and neighbor. Accordingly, freedom and maturity in spiritual direction manifest themselves by an increasing desire on the
part of the directee to both *know* and *do* God's
will in loving response to the God Who is Love.

In their enlightening text *The Practice of
Spiritual Direction*, Barry and Connolly identify
some signs of the presence of resistance in a
person such as "discouragement, boredom, and
depression."[126] They thoughtfully continue their
treatment of these signs of resistance teaching,
"Doubts about the reality of prayer and the
possibility of ever knowing whether one has
experienced God can be manifestations of

---

[125] Congregation for the Clergy, *The Priest,
Minister of Divine Mercy*, §108.
[126] Barry and Connolly, *The Practice of Spiritual
Direction*, 86.

resistance. Avoidance of prayer and of appointments with the spiritual director, repeated lateness for appointments, discussions with the director of everything but prayer experience, desires to quit direction, all can be signs of the presence of resistance to God."[127] Because of this, the spiritual director should be vigilant for such signs of resistance in the directee that the director might truly help the directee to develop an authentic freedom that opens him or her to the divine life welling up within!

Spiritual Direction functions somewhat like traffic signs. Each session is like an intersection where the directee meets the director, who gives him or her the direction toward where the directee wishes to go. Of course, the real process involves much more than this overly simplified illustration, but we can easily get the point from such a picture that, as soon as the directee leaves the session, it is completely up to him or her whether to follow the given direction or not. This is the first notion of freedom in spiritual direction.

If the directee follows the right direction, he or she will reach the next intersection in a timely manner and will progress well toward the

---

[127] Ibid., 87.

desired destination. If another route is taken the director can do nothing but wait patiently until the directee arrives ready for the next direction. Here we see that the notion of "freedom of choice" in spiritual direction applies only to the directee and not to the director, who is an agent of the Holy Spirit, and thus is not at liberty to forgo the directee but is in the business of leading him or her, no matter what happens, to a union with the Trinity.

When delays or inability to follow direction becomes clear, the spiritual director must tactfully invite the directee to recognize the pattern that develops and help him or her to identify what may have caused his or her spiritual growth to stall.

Resistance to getting closer to God comes in different forms and often relates to "schema" or the unconscious way people categorize any object and information they run into for practicality, to benefit from it, or in order to protect their selves from its potential harm. Resistance against contemplative prayer, for instance, may take form in falling asleep, trouble focusing and/or to staying still, or having a steady flow of random, unsolicited thoughts entering and exiting the mind the whole time.

The directee might describe that he or she is feeling bored, tired or easily distracted, which may lead to discouragement and shame. There might be an underlying fear, such as a sense of vulnerability before God, which perhaps rooted in the well-intended but unwisely planted image of God during one's childhood. A prolonged delayed of completion of spiritual reading or a repeated excuse for not having enough time might be rooted in a chronic procrastination that requires a better time management or a behavioral therapy.

Fear of change, obsession for or attachment to wealth, a deceiving sense of responsibility that leads one to believe that he or she "has to" do everything because God has given him or her the capacity for carrying such responsibility, which then raises a justification for avoiding taking time off work for spiritual nourishment, avoiding the possibility that God might be calling the person to a religious life, or an inability to genuinely trust that God can *actually* help with one's unique situation. All of these could be manifestations of resistance, and each must be carefully opened and offered to the Holy Spirit in exchange of total abandonment to God, which requires spiritual direction and discernment.

Spiritual directors must never assume knowledge of the source of the directee's problem even when he or she has heard similar stories from other people. Rather, we must respect the stage on which the directee currently stands, for every individual has a unique background, thus a different level of reactivity, sensitivity and tolerance. Different people will respond differently even when facing the same situation.

In addressing resistance against or avoidance of certain direction, the directee must first be helped to recognize the issue and to explore some potential solutions. Spiritual directors can encourage good reasoning and assessment; however, they should not dictate which things must be done. Their task is to direct the directee to the Holy Spirit for guidance, courage, hope and faith in overcoming his or her challenges, so as to free him- or herself from whatever bond has hampered his or her spiritual growth.

The ideal fruit of spiritual direction is an ever-deepening relationship with God. Therefore, having an open-mindedness or a sense of freedom to rely on God's omnipresence as source and summit in one's life will manifest a perpetual desire for more of a good thing. Being open (disposition) to the Holy Spirit's movement to spiritual direction and to formation in perfection is vital for His holy will. "The authenticity of the spiritual life will be seen by the harmony that exists between the counsels that have been sought and received, and a life that is lived in practical coherence to these."[128]

Examination of conscience is very useful in tapping into God's will as a sort of fraternal partnership between the Holy Spirit and the participant. "The Christian must always enjoy complete freedom and responsibility as a fundamental characteristic to his or her life and action"[129] to avoid a static, pointless and irrelevant pursuit for spiritual progress.

But spiritual direction can stumble from time to time because of underlying resistance or self-images that make it harder to describe one's experiences (counter-movement) with a contemplative attitude and docile demeanor. A spiritual director should gently encourage a directee to see into his or her "pattern of approach to life and prayer." [130] With the art of spiritual direction, a director through dialogue can sharpen the focal point of a directee's aim to

---

[128] Congregation for the Clergy, *The Priest, Minister of Divine Mercy*, §108.

[129] Ibid.

[130] Barry, *Spiritual Direction and the Encounter with God*, 104.

experience the closeness of God by illuminating negative determinants that are blocking spiritual growth and the sense of freedom to relate to God as a friend and not as a foe.

"Resistance often crystallizes around some kind of secret: something I don't want God or my director to know." [131] Therefore an experienced director tries to help directees through Q & A sessions to see one instance of resistance as part of a larger pattern in life and help him or her bring more of him- or herself before God for help. Uncovering motives and history behind resistance opens the hatchway to understanding the "ambivalence" [132] (contradictory attitudes or feelings toward an object, person, or action) of their own action and desire that's preventing their personal movement of spiritual growth.

Through reflection, a directee realizes the reality of his or her life (stoppages) and measures it against his or her particular fixation against the level of a freedom for verses a freedom from. Therefore, this allows a directee to dive deeper into particular responses proper to him or her and God on a one-to-one basis. Rather than emphasizing the fruit, the tenacity of spiritual direction should cultivate an atmo-

---

[131] Ibid.

[132] Ibid., 102.

sphere of openness that examines the root causation that limits the idea of surrender to the process of contemplative introspection, prayer and the attitude needed in acquiring an ever-greater relationship with God.

Change must occur in self-image if a close relationship is to develop intimately with the Holy Spirit. Personality patterns can be deep-seated and disorganized resulting from early childhood experiences. These images are signs that a perceptive director should pick up on to help prevent the progression of self-image analysis and one's vulnerabilities to continually and systematically distort a directee's wanting of a "good spirit" as the zenith of joy, happiness and everlasting peace.

Openness to God is a fundamental charac-teristic of spiritual direction. Fruitful spiritual direction is characterized by the directee's growing more open to God and His will. In order to do so, he or she should be free from im-pediments or resistances. In Christ, the directee can be free from these things in order to be "free for" God and others. But what are these things which cause people to resist God? What are some signs that the directee needs to work on being "freer for" Christ and others?

One of the most important things to note is that these resistances are natural and normal.

Human persons live in a constantly changing world. We have grown up in various situations with varying levels of healthy or unhealthy relationships. Our past experiences will color and affect our relationships to God and others. New ideas of God or of ourselves will be difficult to process and accept.

As many people as there are in the world, there will be many unique situations of resistance to God and change in the spiritual life. It is natural to grow and change only when faced with the challenges presented by difficult and anxiety-producing ideas of events which will naturally cause resistance in the directee. The directee and director should expect them and be prepared for them.

Some signs of resistance include things like discouragement, boredom and depression.[133] Discouragement can be caused by a lack of spiritual progress or the discovery of an incredibly difficult or challenging spiritual truth by directees about themselves or God. Boredom can result when the directee is avoiding or resisting tackling one spiritual challenge so that other topics hold less interest. Depression[134] can

[133] Barry and Connolly, *The Practice of Spiritual Direction*, 86.

[134] Depression can also be the manifestation of another form of resistance. So, it can cause

result when anxiety and fear take over as the directee resists facing a difficult topic or idea.

Spiritual direction actually starts and ends with others exchanging ideas, fears, sorrows and personal counter-movements to spiritual progress in relationship to themselves with others and with God. If a resistance is not recognized by the directee yet, it's not wise to tackle it head on in an aggressive manner until the directee is ready to really deal with it. Especially in earlier sessions as the two are getting to know each other, "tackling" a problem could lead to the halting of further direction if the directee does not like the aggressive approach of the director. Other signs of resistance include a constantly cheery experience of prayer, persistent repetition of response, falling asleep in prayer and doubts about having ever experienced God.[135]

A secret the directee keeps from God and the director is particularly noteworthy and can be a manifestation of resistance. Resistance happens when the directee begins to become aware of it

---

resistance to spiritual growth but also can be a manifestation of resistance as the directee experiences frustration, anger and sadness at not progressing spiritually or in encountering something he or she doesn't want to deal with.

[135] Ibid., 86-87.

and wants to avoid acknowledging it to God or the director. Of course, God knows the secret, so it must be shared with God, but their question is whether it is necessary to tell it to the director in order to overcome the resistance and move along smoothly with the direction.

We have known instances where it was first necessary for directees to be able to tell their director the secret before they could tell it to God. We also know instances in which the secret was shared with God and not with the director. In these cases, however, it seemed that the director needed to help the directee recognize that the "secret" was blocking progress in prayer and thus help him or her tell the whole truth to God."[136]

The director should "keep their sense of humor and an awareness of their own fallibility. The signs of resistance are only that— signs, not proof."[137] Temperamental differences can also be another source of resistance.[138]

---

[136] Ibid., 104.

[137] Ibid., 98.

[138] The difference between the temperaments of the director and the directee could cause the directee to resist any guidance or questions from the director or have a bias or prejudice to the questions or suggestions from the director. There could be differences in temperament from moment to moment

Resistances should be first recognized for what they are and reflected upon. Harmony should exist between the directee and the director first—lest a confrontation ensue. Then the spiritual director can encourage the directee to work through the resistance, beginning where it first manifests itself on the surface. The directee should take full responsibility for his or her actions, not laying guilt or blame on the director for the situation. The director should recognize that it is not his or her job to "fix" the directee or to give direction as to the nature or cause of the resistance but simply help guide the directee to work through it with assistance from the Holy Spirit.

---

in the directee. This could also signal the directee is experiencing resistance. The directee may react with anger, frustration or sadness to a topic brought up in spiritual direction. It would be important to accept this reaction and emotion and approach it as any other resistance. It is key to recognize the differences in the directee's reactions in order to properly discern the resistance and its cause.

Role Play

In working on community projects, one brother always dominates the discussion. He expects his brothers to immediately understand and join in with his plan. If others try to share their ideas or make additional suggestions, the dominant brother becomes defensive and begins to disengage from the group. In planning a surprise birthday party, this dynamic occurs.

Another brother, who is sick and tired of this dynamic, loses his temper and tells the domineering brother exactly what he thinks about the brother's vision. The domineering brother looks hurt, says nothing and leaves the room. The domineering brother who was terribly hurt could no longer participate in any community project because he finds it difficult to understand why someone can be that mean. He comes to you as a community director for a way forward.

What would *you* say to your directee?

XII

Conclusion

Spiritual direction is indeed built on trust and is ordered towards concrete action in the spiritual life. Accountability is an essential ingredient in spiritual direction. The aspect of accountability in spiritual direction is a great gift and blessing since it encourages us to not only "talk the talk," but to "walk the walk." Not only does accountability, therefore, suggest the importance of regular spiritual direction, but it further reveals the vital importance of trust, transparency and docility between director and directee.

Spiritual direction must be consistent and ongoing; spiritual direction is not a onetime emergency-room event, since the goal is to not only identify the workings of God in the soul, but to consistently and faithfully correspond throughout the whole of one's life. By regular, ongoing interaction with a spiritual director, he or she can ensure that we actually "practice what we preach."

Spiritual direction focuses on spiritual matters such as spiritual experiences, prayer life and the deepening of one's relationship with God through discernment and exploration of the presence of God in one's life. Placing spiritual direction side-by-side with psychotherapy and the Sacrament of reconciliation, we highlight the difference in method and end goal from the other two.

Just like any real conversation between friends, prayer necessitates that we listen for the Lord's voice and the promptings of the indwelling Paraclete in our souls. Spiritual direction is no different since we have a temptation to want to do all the talking. Such a great benefit, however, is to be had from active listening, which manifests to the directee that we truly seek to enter his or her experience/ situation in order to understand! To be effective spiritual directors, then, we must learn how to listen, to what the directee does and does not say, that we might help him or her to more clearly know and do God's perfect will.

Our world today is so filled with constant noise that it is easy to lose our way. In addition to noise, there is great activity in the constant hustle and bustle of daily life. How important, therefore, to make ample use of spiritual direction to discern what noise is from the world, from ourselves, perhaps from the devil, and what is truly God's voice speaking gently, softly to the soul.

Moreover, spiritual direction reminds us of the importance of slowing down to be mindful of the divine presence throughout each moment of the day. Spiritual direction orientates us towards the God Who is love and Who wills to enter into relationship with His creatures, diffusing His goodness and drawing us into His divine life.

The ultimate end of spiritual direction is, as Jesus commanded, to "love the Lord your God with all your heart, and with all your soul, and with all your mind, and with all your strength" and to "love your neighbor as yourself" (Mk. 12: 30– 31). Spiritual direction is about developing a love relationship with God that inevitably spills into all other areas of our lives.

Without a sincere desire for holiness, spiritual direction would never have a specific objecttive or purpose in Christian life since God calls each man and woman to holiness. The central aim of spiritual direction is to help guide the directee to purposefully, consistently and substantively grow in his or her relationship with God and neighbor.

A spiritual director must possess a warmth about him or her that not only welcomes the directee, but also makes the directee feel safe and loved with authentic Christian love. After all, the topics regularly discussed in spiritual direction are deeply personal: our relationship with God and neighbor, our prayer life, the pursuit of virtue and eradication of vice. In order for the directee to feel at ease to humbly and candidly open his or her soul, the warmth of the director can really help to make spiritual direction not only productive, but also a joyful experience.

The human spiritual director must be a man or woman who has the heart and qualities of Jesus Christ and allows him or herself to be directed, which means to listen and hear God speak in order to be guided by the Spirit through the direction process while helping another soul. We must never take our own experience as the norm for everyone else. One of the most difficult challenges with which to deal in our relationship with others is acknowledging the uniqueness or peculiarity of one's life experience from another person's even when they experience something very similar.

If, for instance, a director had in the past struggled with alcoholism and was able to overcome this problem within a relatively short period, he or she should never judge a directee who keeps failing in the attempt to free him/- or herself from the similar problem. For there must be differences in the cultural, economic, educational, genetic and other backgrounds between the director and the directee that account for the inability of the directee to overcome very similar problems in the same amount of time as the director could.

The right attitude will be to have compassion for the directee and to support him or her with even greater love. Sometimes tough love is required and rightly so. The main idea is to wish what is good for the directee.

The relationship between the spiritual director and directee, grounded in our holy Catholic faith and necessarily built upon mutual trust and respect, would become unhealthy if it became physically, sexually, or emotionally dependent. If the relationship were to go in this direction, "the relationship should be terminated immediately."[139]

If you find yourself getting emotionally attracted to the directee, humility suggests that you would need to end the relationship since at that point not only would you be putting yourself and your vocation in a potentially dangerous situation, but you would also be compromising your ability to help the directee discern God's

---

[139] Burke and Bartunek, *Navigating the Interior Life*, 44.

Will and enter into an ever richer relationship with the Triune God since you would no longer be able to be objective and disinterested.

God's plan for our salvation was made manifest in the life of Jesus Christ as He proceeds from the Father and through the Holy Spirit. The Spirit directs the church with its members, and based on this, both the director and the directee have every reason to say "Yes" to the Spirit and to the teachings of the Church in the sacraments and the word of God in the scriptures through a life deeply rooted in prayer. They must fully let the Holy Spirit take total and complete charge in all their undertakings.

The director should fade into the background by fostering the relationship between the directee and the Paraclete. Here he must strive to actively listen to the directee during their regular sessions of spiritual direction and to urge the directee on to greater growth. The director does this by listening to the directee and inviting the directee to persevere and grow in his or her relationship with our God Who is a Trinity of Persons.

It is important to be reminded of the importance of a certain disinterestedness on the part of the director who is called to care deeply for the directee as a child of God but to not "get in the way." The director is best able to fade away, then, by being him- or herself a person of prayer, sensitive to the voice of God, and by seeking to be God's instrument in spiritual direction.

The holiness to which we have been called by baptism is one since it has its source in our God Who is one. However, the spiritual direction given to a priest is necessarily distinct from that offered to a consecrated religious or a member of the lay faithful. This is logical enough since the challenges faced by a priest in his parish life are necessarily distinct from the crosses born by a cloistered religious or a wife with a hectic family life.

Everyone in this list is seeking to be transformed in God and to enter ever more fully into the divine life by grace, but each has a distinct vocation with different crosses. There will be much in common for sure, but there are differences, too. Spiritual direction, however, must not cease once we have discerned our vocations, but rather must continue throughout our lives: nurturing our faith, renewing our hope and enkindling our charity. Every spiritual direction session is to dispose the directee to be as comfortable as possible.

Prayer is an essential part of spiritual direction. It does not matter when it is said, but if not it loses its essential ingredient. Spiritual direction is about professional friendship between a director and his directee which generally should start on a positive note and progresses to a more challenging area of the directee's life. Serving as a spiritual director is a great responsibility, but it is also a humbling experience of encountering the hand of God in another person's life and helping that person to not only recognize God's hand but act according to God's will.

While spiritual direction can undoubtedly be tiring, take practice and sometimes feel like another responsibility of our priestly life, we must never cease to radiate a recognizable warmth to the directee that makes him or her know that he or she is loved, cherished and respected as a precious child of God. Though indiscriminate use of psychology is discouraged for spiritual direction, its application to help better understand a directee can be quite valuable.

In short, psychologism or spiritualism must be avoided in the ministry of spiritual direction. A sign of growth in spiritual direction is a life that is centered in Christ and has a strong foundation in many contributing factors in which God allows the individual to grow. Prayer, humility and sacrifice are but three things that help an individual discern and show signs of growth. The more dedicated one is to God in his prayer life, the more he wants to praise Him and communicate with Him. This will allow a person to have a deeper relationship with God. Humility reveals that a person must always be willing to place God and His will before our own so we may be able to properly serve Him.

The director is invited to help the directee understand the resistances he or she places between him or her and God and neighbor and to then respond freely with an abundance of charity and in a mature manner.

This finally takes us back to where we started which is the original definition of spiritual direction, which is a sustained attempt at leading a person to an understanding and an acceptance of self, thus helping that person strip away the barriers that impede the action of the Holy Spirit in him, that is, to a greater opening to the Holy Spirit and His movements within the person.

It is a sustained attempt in the sense that there must be some sort of regularity, permanence, continuity and consistency if it is going to be true spiritual direction. If it is something occasionally done, it may qualify for pastoral counseling but not spiritual direction. It is a sustained attempt at leading a person and not pushing a person. If spiritual direction is a training in freedom, then the director is not to push his directee or impose his ideas or opinions on him. It is a gentle leading of an individual to a full opening of the self.

About the Author

Fr. Dominic Ugoo Anaeto is a priest of the Catholic Diocese of Nnewi in Nigeria. He holds a License in Spirituality from Gregorian University in Rome, a Doctorate in Pastoral Theology from the Lateran University also in Rome, and a diploma from the Christian Institute for the Study of Human Sexuality at the Catholic Theological Union in Chicago, Illinois. He is a certified counselor on topics related to Human Development and Human Sexuality. He has served as the Director of the Master of Arts in Pastoral Studies program at Holy Apostles College & Seminary in Cromwell, CT, and as Director of Pastoral Formation at St. Mary's Seminary in Houston, TX.

www.ingramcontent.com/pod-product-compliance
Lightning Source LLC
Chambersburg PA
CBHW022006090426
42741CB00007B/918

*9 7 8 1 9 5 0 1 0 8 1 4 5 *